CRUISING
ALASKA

5TH EDITION

CRUISING ALASKA

5TH EDITION

A TRAVELER'S GUIDE TO CRUISING ALASKAN WATERS & DISCOVERING THE INTERIOR

LARRY H. LUDMER

HUNTER

HUNTER PUBLISHING, INC.
130 Campus Drive, Edison, NJ 08818
732-225-1900; 800-255-0343; Fax 732-417-1744
hunterp@bellsouth.net

Ulysses Travel Publications
4176 Saint-Denis, Montréal, Québec
Canada H2W 2M5
514-843-9882, ext. 2232; Fax 514-843-9448

The Boundary, Wheatley Road, Garsington
Oxford, OX44 9EJ England
01865-361122; Fax 01865-361133

ISBN 1-58843-115-0
© 2001 Larry H. Ludmer

Cover image: Alsec Bay & Mount Fairweather Tatshenshini, AK
Rex A. Bryngelson, Adventure Photo.

Maps by Kim André © 2001 Hunter Publishing

8 5 6 7

Acknowledgments

As always, I would like to thank Bonnie Crosby of Cruise Holidays of Henderson/Las Vegas for her assistance in coordinating the gathering of important information on the various cruise ships traveling to Alaska. In addition, the prompt and courteous assistance provided by the media relations departments of the cruise lines is greatly appreciated. Worthy of special mention in the latter group are Denise Seomin of Princess; Maureen Camandona of Glacier Bay Tours & Cruises; Dennis Myrick of World Explorer Cruises; and Gayle Kohmetscher of Clipper Cruises. Thanks to all.

Contents

Contents

MAPS

Introduction

Alaska is far and away the largest state in the United States, dwarfing even Texas. Its area is equal to one-fifth that of the entire lower 48 states. One can cite endless statistics to impress you with its size and variety, but numbers cannot capture the beauty and magic of Alaska; it has to be visited in order to truly appreciate all of its outstanding features.

Because of its size, you won't be able to see all of Alaska on one single visit. Moreover, a significant portion of the state's interior is not readily accessible, except to the most experienced wilderness adventurers. This, however, shouldn't discourage anyone interested in nature's beauty from venturing north. There is still much that can easily be visited.

The Way to See Alaska

The most heavily visited region of Alaska lies along the long strip of coast from just beyond the Canadian border at Ketchikan north to Yakutat Bay and then west along the south coast bordering the Gulf of Alaska. This is a land of high and virtually impenetrable mountain ranges and mighty glaciers – a rugged terrain. Roads, where they exist at all, generally run only for a few miles in either direction of the major towns and then end. Boats are the primary means of getting from place to place. They serve as a lifeline to many of these remote communities.

The other main touring area is a roughly straight line that extends north from the city of Anchorage, past Denali National Park and finally reaching Fairbanks. While this area can be reached either by car or via the Alaska Railroad, it is, for most visitors from the Lower 48, second in importance to the sights along the coast.

A trip to Alaska is, for many people, a once-in-a-lifetime experience, and a cruise is without doubt one of the most extraordinary ways to see it. It affords you the best scenery while floating on icy blue waters and gives you the opportunity to jump ship, hop on a flightseeing plane, and take a different look at the wonders that surround you. But a formal cruise on a big liner isn't the only way to explore Alaska's coastal waters. A number of smaller ships make limited runs in specific areas. They often stop at places the larger ships never get to visit. Another possibility is the Alaska Marine Highway, a system of ferries that serve virtually all the important coastal towns as well as points in the Gulf of Alaska. We'll take a look at each of these methods as well as a few others, but will devote the most attention to the cruise ships because the biggest number of Alaska visitors choose that method. And there's no denying that for an overview during a first-time visit, it probably is the best way to go.

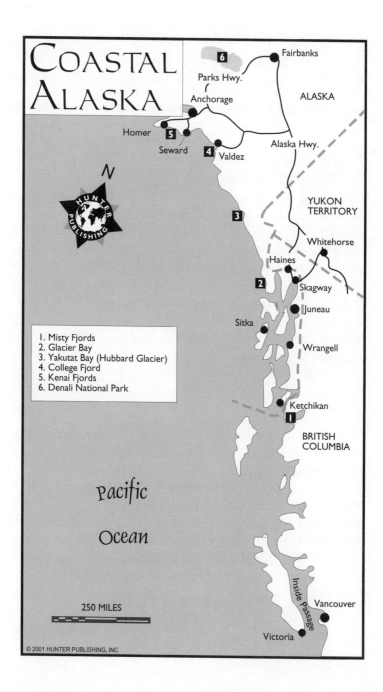

COASTAL ALASKA

1. Misty Fjords
2. Glacier Bay
3. Yakutat Bay (Hubbard Glacier)
4. College Fjord
5. Kenai Fjords
6. Denali National Park

Fairbanks

Parks Hwy.

Anchorage

ALASKA

Homer

Seward

Valdez

Alaska Hwy.

N

HUNTER PUBLISHING

YUKON
TERRITORY

Whitehorse

Haines

Skagway

Juneau

Sitka

Wrangell

Ketchikan

BRITISH
COLUMBIA

Pacific

Ocean

Inside Passage

Vancouver

250 MILES

Victoria

© 2001 HUNTER PUBLISHING, INC

Setting Priorities: Best Cruise Ship vs. Best Itinerary

In most instances people who are going on cruise ships select a destination and then try to find the "best" ship for them. Types of cuisine and the age of the crowd on a particular ship are among the many factors that can influence your final decision. The ship's itinerary is almost an afterthought in many cases. This is fine for cruises to the Caribbean (after all, a beach is a beach and one marketplace begins to look a lot like another after a few port calls). The same can be said for some other places where the primary purpose of the trip is often the *cruise experience* itself rather than the *destination*. This is not the case in Alaska. If you decide to cruise to Alaska it is more than likely that the reason for your cruise is to see the wonderful sights of America's last frontier. While the atmosphere, luxuries and activities on board will, no doubt, add to your enjoyment, the fact is that many people will consider those aspects of the cruise of secondary importance. Therefore, it is more important to select the ship based on its destinations (i.e., the ports of call and what scenic cruising is included).

Ship itineraries vary considerably. To cite an example, some of the larger cruise ships are too big to navigate in areas that are of primary importance to a first-time Alaska visitor. Some concentrate only on the Inside Passage, while others travel on to the Gulf of Alaska. (All these options will be discussed at length later.) There aren't any "bad" cruise ships traveling to Alaska, so the single most important factor in selecting a ship is to identify the one whose itinerary most closely resembles the itinerary you would make if you could travel at will.

The Right Cruise For You

The Alaskan Cruise Market

There's little doubt that the Alaskan cruise market has been one of the fastest-growing segments of the travel industry for several years running. The last couple of years have seen an unprecedented pace of change. In general, the major cruise lines have been placing their newest and largest ships on Alaskan routes. This has increased passenger capacity and, to some degree, has helped to keep costs down. On the other hand, many of the ships are now so large that they are unable to sail into quite a few of the beautiful but tight bays of the Inside Passage. Also, when a couple of mega-liners tie up at a small town such as Skagway, it can create a severe strain on the limited facilities of such communities. At the other end of the scale is a big increase in the number of "alternative" cruise vessels – ships that used to be grouped under a heading called the *explorer* class, but are now simply referred to as small ships. What this all means for you is that there is a greater choice of ships than ever before – all the more reason to go through the list that follows with great care. The cruise industry has also seen mergers and consolidations along with new players in Alaska and the departure of some familiar names. The list of cruise operators in Alaska for 2001 reads quite differently than in previous years.

Traditional Cruise Lines

CARNIVAL CRUISE LINES

The "fun" line is an immensely successful cruise line with a devoted following, especially among family travelers. Their experience and reputation have been developed primarily in the Caribbean market. They have been in the Alaskan market since 1996 and, although not a major player in terms of the number of ships available up north, the feedback we've received has been mostly of a highly positive nature.

CELEBRITY CRUISES

This is another big name in the cruise industry that entered the Alaskan foray in 1996. They, too, used the Caribbean sector as their stairway to fame and fortune, but now have two thoroughly modern and luxurious ships serving Alaska along with a host of cruising experience in the luxury level. This line has consistently received high praise in cruise passenger surveys and definitely is a more upscale experience than some of the larger cruise lines. Celebrity was acquired by Royal Caribbean Cruise lines a several years ago but Celebrity operates independently and passengers won't even be aware of the merger.

CRYSTAL CRUISES

The last of the three "Cs" (it used to be four, but Cunard no longer goes to Alaska), Crystal also began sailing to Alaska in 1996. That was a very good year, it seems, for Alaska cruises.

It marked the realization by the industry that there was gold in the Alaskan market. Crystal has also received favorable reviews from Alaskan passengers and it's no wonder – their ships are among the most beautiful on the high seas. For 2001, Crystal will again be sending the *Harmony* into the Alaskan waters.

HOLLAND AMERICA LINE

No one has been showing Alaska to the world longer than Holland America and, in many ways, they remain as dean of this region. In fact, HAL has been showing Alaska to the world for more than 50 years, so few can match their knowledge and expertise. With six ships sailing to Alaska on their 2001 schedule, they are the largest carrier in this market in terms of the number of vessels. Since many of their ships are somewhat smaller than their biggest competitor (Princess), they are in second place in terms of total passenger capacity. The last few years have seen the introduction of several newer vessels into their traditionally styled fleet. Holland America has a five-star rating and they are considered to be one of the best cruise lines in the business. Their Westours affiliate makes cruise/land packages easy to book. These packages are, apparently, flawlessly organized. You can choose from almost 30 different cruise-tours that range all the way up to adventure travel. For those seeking an extensive array of shore excursions or pre- and post-cruise tours, Holland America is at or near the top in this area. The company also operates a large number of hotels throughout Alaska under the Westmark banner.

NORWEGIAN CRUISE LINE

Norwegian has one of the best reputations in the cruise industry without getting into the stratosphere pricing range, and their ships are all first rate. They've been serving Alaska since the early 1990s and even longer if you consider that they acquired Royal Cruise Line several years ago. They'll have two

The Right Cruise For You

first-class vessels plying the waters of the Inside Passage and coastal Alaska during 2001. NCL was the first cruise line to establish Seattle as an embarkation point for Alaska cruises. Whether this is a trend that we'll be seeing more of in the future remains to be seen.

PRINCESS CRUISES

The *Love Boat* company is synonymous with cruising to much of the public and they've been introducing luxurious new mega-liners to their fleet at an astonishing rate over the past several years. These wonderful floating palaces give them an edge in the eyes of many people over their biggest rival in Alaska, Holland America. Princess now has primarily newer ships serving Alaska, which have replaced several older and smaller vessels that used to be employed on these routes. That is, of course, a mixed blessing. The huge liners of today are sights to behold but, as mentioned earlier, do have some drawbacks in Alaska's smaller bays and inlets. Some experienced cruisers are also a bit turned off by the tremendous number of passengers on these ships. That not withstanding, Princess is one of the older operators in Alaska and they certainly don't have to take a back seat to Holland America in their experience and knowledge of the Great Land. They, too, have a tremendous number of land-based add-ons. In fact, their Alaska cruise-tour options number in excess of 50! Four of the five ships that will go to Alaska in 2001 are being devoted to the Gulf of Alaska one-way run from Vancouver to Seward. These "Grand Class" ships are joined by one other vessel that will be handling the round-trip Inside Passage run. Princess, like HAL, has acquired a number of lodging establishments throughout Alaska that makes combining land options even easier.

RADISSON SEVEN SEAS CRUISES

An affiliate of the respected Radisson hotel chain, Seven Seas provides a luxury cruise experience beyond what you would get from the mainstream large cruise lines. That's because the ships of this line are much smaller than typical in today's cruise industry. While these ships are especially well suited to Alaska cruising, the down side is that Radisson is much more expensive than the competition. If you can afford the tariff, Radisson is an excellent choice. They've been sailing to Alaska for several years.

ROYAL CARIBBEAN INTERNATIONAL

A mid-sized player in Alaska for quite a few years, Royal Caribbean seems to vary the number of ships it sends to Alaska, as if they're not quite sure how much is enough. Regardless of the numbers, they have a well-deserved reputation and have certainly proven their ability in Alaskan waters. Their 2001 lineup is the largest it's been in some time and includes three ships, all of which are quite new and can be included in the spectacular mega-class of liners.

Other Ship Operators

ALASKA MARINE HIGHWAY SYSTEM

Operating a large fleet of varying size ferries that carry cars and passengers, the Marine Highway offers a more informal way to get around. Their route system, as well as the advantages and disadvantages of this method of seeing Alaska, will be discussed in more detail later, but you should be aware that the ferries are not luxury cruise experiences. There are staterooms available (you can also just occupy deck space), but this is transportation only, not a cruise.

CLIPPER LINE

Clipper is one of the largest and best known "small ship" operators in America, and they've been in Alaska for quite a few years. This is luxury on a more personal level. As you'll see later, the itineraries for Clipper ships (and others in the same class) are quite different than the big liners. In general, they offer a more detailed exploration of a more limited area than the larger ships. Small ships aren't less expensive than the more prestigious mega-liners, though. In fact, without the economies of scale, they can often be even higher priced.

GLACIER BAY TOURS & CRUISES

Similar to the Clipper line and several others, these lines appeal to the individual who is looking for a more in-depth experience. That, and their smaller ships, are the strong points. Although Clipper may have more routes throughout America than any other line, it is Glacier Bay Tours that has the largest variety of Alaskan itineraries as well as the most ships in this class. With that level of experience you can count on a first-rate Alaskan wilderness adventure.

LINBLAD EXPEDITIONS

This company was one of the first to offer "soft adventure" travel that calls for lots of activity but without the necessity of being in top physical shape or having specialized outdoor skills. They were also ecologically friendly before it became in vogue to be so. Their Alaska cruises are all on small ships that feature Zodiac rafts for detailed exploration on both land and sea. While their vessels aren't luxurious, they do offer all of the comforts associated with first-class small ships.

WORLD EXPLORER CRUISES

This company offers a cross between the traditional cruise liners and the small ships. Their vessel is an older one that has been plying Alaska's waters for many years. It offers a casual and detailed journey that appeals to many people. If you feel a bit intimidated by the mega-liners but aren't sure if you want to spend a week on a tiny ship, then World Explorer Cruises could be a suitable in-between solution for you. Their expertise in Alaska certainly is equal to that of the bigger competitors.

The Ships

Alaska used to be a place that only a few people visited. But the 1990s saw an enormous increase in the number of people flocking to the 49th state and the cruise lines have been instrumental in bringing about this influx of visitors. There are more ships cruising Alaska now than ever before – new ships, huge liners, smaller and more intimate luxury cruise ships. While the pace of addition has begun to slow, the latest trend is for even bigger ships. Thus, even without the introduction of more ships, the number of visitors continues to grow. In 2001 there will be a total of 21 ships that we characterize as "large" sailing to Alaska, and they can carry a total in excess of 34,000 passengers.

One definite advantage to the bargain cruiser is that the heavy competition tends to keep prices down. So, too, do the larger ships, which have a lower per-person operating cost than do smaller ones. The choice is large enough to find what you're looking for, but the variety can often be confusing. In this section we'll shed as much light as possible on what's available by providing you with capsule descriptions of all the ships currently sailing Alaskan waters. You can pick out your favorites and then examine their itineraries in a subsequent section. If you've ever browsed through cruise line brochures you know that every ship is presented as being the best, most luxurious or most beautiful. Well, we know that can't be true; some have to be nicer than others.

Every large cruise ship features three full meals a day, a late-night buffet, plus snacks (that can often be a meal in themselves) throughout the day. Attractive shops and chic boutiques, a casino, health club or gymnasium (often including a

The Right Cruise For You

spa), bars, lounges and a nightclub with entertainment are also a certainty. Therefore, our descriptions may sometimes omit this information to avoid redundancy. The same is true for activities – a full slate will be offered each and every day on every ship. Staterooms all have private bath, often with a full tub. Rooms are equipped with all of the amenities you'd expect to find in a fine hotel.

We have mentioned that bigger isn't always better because of the tight navigational restrictions in some parts of Alaskan waters and because of lengthy lines that can form on bigger ships for buffets and port tenders. The latter will be of varying importance to different people based on their own personal temperament. In the listings to follow, facts include the length of the ship and the number of passengers it carries. While no comment will be made under each ship as to how that might affect your experience, we offer these general guidelines. Regarding ship length, less than 750 feet is best for Alaska cruising; between 700 and 825 feet is adequate; and 825 feet or longer could definitely limit access to some areas of scenic cruising. As far as passenger counts are concerned, under 1,000 is generally not a problem, crowd-wise. Between 1,000 and 1,500 is adequate; and more than 1,500 has the potential for big lines and long waits. Of course, the number of passengers alone is not the only criteria for determining ease of access. A lot does depend on how well the ship is designed, the number of tenders, and the organizational skills of the crew. But, the raw numbers are still quite useful as a starting point for your consideration.

Please note that the information given in this book is based on data available at press time, but cruise lines generally make plans far in advance so there is always the possibility of a last-minute change in ship and/or itinerary. The ships listed here are all scheduled to be in Alaskan waters during the 2001 season.

Many of the information categories for each ship in the listings that follow are self-explanatory. However, a few points need to be made in advance concerning the nature of the information that is contained in several of them.

▶ Built: Indicates the year when the ship was actually first placed into service.

▶ Passengers: If you read other sources of information about these ships you may well encounter higher passenger capacities than are shown in this book. The reason for that is that every ship has a maximum allowable passenger load as determined by the Coast Guard. In practice, however, the cruise lines impose a much lower limitation. On selected sailings it is possible that there will be more passengers on board than is shown due to the number of third guests in a room, children with parents in the same room, and so forth. However, the listed passenger capacity in this book will still be closer to the actual amount than the prescribed Coast Guard limits.

▶ Stateroom Size: This is the square footage range for the smallest to largest; suites are categorized separately when that information is available. Keep in mind that most first-class hotels these days have an average size in the neighborhood of around 500 square feet – something you won't see in the non-suite category on a cruise ship.

▶ Price Range: This indicates the published rates (i.e., the brochure rates) for the highest and lowest priced accommodations for the length of the trip shown. The peak or high season in Alaska is almost always July and August, regardless of the cruise line. All prices are exclusive of personal expenditures, port charges and tipping, except if in-

The Right Cruise For You

dicated otherwise. Please note that at press time the state of Alaska was considering imposing a $50 per person tax on all cruises beginning in 2001. If this is enacted, you will have to add this amount to all the prices shown. On the other hand, the costs as listed do not reflect early booking or other discounts offered by the cruise line or some cruise travel agencies. These can often be significant (at least 10% and often greater). Tipping can be an expensive proposition too, and must be calculated into your budget. A few lines have instituted a no-tipping policy. Of course, gratuities for the crew are still figured into the price. In Alaska, the only lines currently offering a tip-free atmosphere are Holland America and Radisson Seven Seas.

For some strange reason the cruise lines have different ways of counting how long their cruises are. To be consistent, we have based the length on the following criteria: (1) Only the cruise portion of the itinerary is counted; (2) the length in days is considered to be the number of nights on board plus one. Thus, if you spend seven nights on board the cruise will be listed as being eight days in length.

Large Cruise Liners

⚓ CARNIVAL SPIRIT (Carnival Cruise Lines)

Built: 2001	Registry: Panama
Length: 960 feet	Gross Tonnage: 84,000
Passengers: 2,124	Passenger Decks: 12
Staterooms: 1,062	Stateroom Size: 160-415 sq. ft.
Crew Size: 920	Passenger/Crew Ratio: 2.3:1
Officers: Italian	Crew: International

MEAL ARRANGEMENTS: The stunning two-level main dining room has early and late seatings for all meals. Alternative dining options include the casual Lido eatery (all meals) and a specialty restaurant. The latter extends from the ship's smokestack out over the edge of the ship's atrium.

CRUISE STYLE: There are one or two formal nights per cruise and an equal number of informal nights. The remainder of the evenings are casual.

PRICE RANGE: The fares for the eight-day Vancouver to Seward itinerary are from $1,919 to $2,869 for regular staterooms and from $3,269 to $3,669 for suites. The same length Inside Passage cruise has a price range of $1,579 to $$2,529 for regular staterooms while suites go from $2,929 up to $3,329.

Setting the standard for Carnival lines' future ships, the brand new *Spirit's* public areas are highlighted by the expansive and dazzling multi-level atrium lobby. Everything is high-tech, from the ship's environmental systems to the engines – the latter allowing this ship to reach higher speeds than most other contemporary cruise liners. But the behind-the-scenes details will be of far less interest to travelers than the décor and styling of the ship, both of which are nothing short of spectacular. Carnival has taken those portions of its "Fantasy" and "Destiny" class ships that were best received by the sailing public and incorporated them into this ship. Despite the large number of passengers, the *Spirit* has one of the best space ratios of any large ship going to Alaska. The generously sized staterooms are thoughtfully designed and the majority of them have their own private veranda.

Of course, this ship has the full range of recreational, socializing and entertainment facilities that you would expect. This includes several swimming pools, one of which has its own 72-foot-long spiral water slide! We don't know how many Alaska-bound passengers will be able to take advantage of it but we can assume that any small children traveling with you will be well looked after at "Camp Carnival" in the ship's "Fun House."

⚓ CRYSTAL HARMONY *(Crystal Cruises)*

Built: 1990
Length: 790 feet
Passengers: 940
Staterooms: 480
Crew Size: 545
Officers: Scandinavian/Japanese

Registry: Bahamas
Gross Tonnage: 49,400
Passenger Decks: 8
Stateroom Size:183-271 sq. ft.;
suites to 948 sq. ft.
Passenger/Crew Ratio: 1.7:1
Crew: European/International

MEAL ARRANGEMENTS: The main dining room (called the Crystal Dining Room) has early and late seatings for all meals but more flexible dining is available at a number of other restaurants. Among these are a Japanese and Italian restaurant, but there is also a bistro, an indoor/outdoor café and an outdoor grill. At the latter you will find food items that appeal to the younger traveler – namely hot dogs and hamburgers.

CRUISE STYLE: There are two formal nights on each cruise and three informal nights. The remainder of the evenings are casual. It should be noted that Crystal Cruises is among the more formal operators going to Alaska.

PRICE RANGE: Stateroom prices for the 11-night cruise range from $4,720 to $7,840 on all sailings with suite prices beginning at $10,990 and rising to a maximum of $18,080.

A beautiful liner that is well regarded by cruise veterans, the *Crystal Harmony* is highlighted by the two-story high Crystal Plaza atrium lobby with hand-cut glass sculptures; it even has a waterfall. The domed Vista Observation Lounge is a great place to watch the scenery pass by, and shoppers will delight at the large Avenue of the Stars arcade. The ship features several lounges, a cabaret-style nightclub, large casino, 227-seat theater, and one of the most extensive fitness centers afloat. The entertainment program is extensive and includes a production show, cabaret, '50s theme show and recitals by classical musicians. Over half of the ship's staterooms have private verandas. Each has a large separate sitting area and refrigerator with mini-bar. For a real luxury experience try the Penthouse Deck, where each suite has its own jacuzzi and butler service.

Regardless of which accommodations you select, the *Crystal Harmony's* service is considered to be among the best of the ships operated by the major cruise lines. This should not be surprising in view of their excellent passenger/crew ratio.

⚓ DAWN PRINCESS *(Princess Cruises)*

Built: 1996	Registry: Britain
Length: 856 feet	Gross Tonnage: 77,000
Passengers: 1,950	Passenger Decks: 10
Staterooms: 1,011	Stateroom Size: 175 sq. ft.
Crew Size: 900	Passenger/Crew Ratio: 2.2:1
Officers: European	Crew: International

MEAL ARRANGEMENTS: There are early and late seatings for all three meals in either of the two main dining rooms. However, this ship offers a tremendous variety of 24-hour dining options that include a pizzeria, casual grill, food court, buffet and even alternative restaurants.

CRUISE STYLE: There is one formal night and two informal nights. The remainder are casual. However, because of the large number of dining options it is possible to go casual every night for those who are averse to the tie and jacket routine.

PRICE RANGE: The basic fares begin at $1,699 for the eight-day cruise, while the best stateroom will cost you $3,149. Suites are available beginning at $4,099 and rise to a high of $5,079.

The *Dawn Princess* is one of a group of new "Grand Class" liners that Princess has introduced over the past several years. Along with this ship, there are several other family members that are scheduled for Alaskan sailings in 2001. These sister ships are the *Ocean, Sea* and *Sun Princesses.* While some of the names of restaurants and other public areas may vary from ship to another they are, for all intents and purposes, identical ships. And, what ships they are!

Grand Class liners feature a space-per-passenger ratio that exceeds the industry average (as do the staterooms). These ships are easily becoming recognizable to cruise goers. Despite their

The Right Cruise For You

massive size, these all-white ships have a certain gracefulness and implicit beauty about them. The range of facilities befits their size stature as well. In fact, what you'll find is an abundance of what is usually found on a large liner. For instance, there are two separate showrooms and five different places to eat. The large fitness center is glass enclosed and suspended between two decks. Children's facilities and activities are numerous. And since this is going to be an Alaska cruise, you want plenty of good vantage points to watch the scenery go by. For that, there are wrap-around decks and plenty of lounges with excellent viewing conditions. All of the staterooms are of a nice size and are beautifully decorated. A large percentage of the outside rooms have their own private balcony.

⚓ INFINITY (Celebrity Cruises)

Built: 2001	Registry: Liberia
Length: 965 feet	Gross Tonnage: 91,000
Passengers: 1,950	Passenger Decks: 11
Staterooms: 1,021	Stateroom Size: 170-1,432 sq.ft.
Crew Size: 997	Passenger/Crew Ratio: 1.9:1
Officers: Greek	Crew: International

MEAL ARRANGEMENTS: The main dining room has early and late seatings for all meals. Alternative dining arrangements with flexible seating include buffets for breakfast and lunch and a number of specialty restaurants, including a room called the SS United States with its own dine-in wine cellar and the much more casual but delightful Trellis Restaurant.

CRUISE STYLE: There are generally two formal evenings and two informal evenings on this line, making it among the more formal of Alaskan cruises. All the remaining nights are casual.

PRICE RANGE: Regular stateroom prices begin at $1,749 for the seven-night cruise and rise to $3,449. Suite fares range from $5,779 through $11,329. Celebrity has the same theoretical price range for the entire cruising season but bigger discounts are definitely easier to get during fringe periods. Their May and September positioning cruises are actually longer but cost less for those willing to brave the weather possibilities.

This book went to press prior to *Infinity's* inaugural cruise so there no public feedback was available. However, based on information provided by the cruise line, the *Infinity* will take its place among the most notable vessels in Alaska. The amount of wood, marble, etched glass and polished granite that have been employed in decorating the interior grab your attention for sure. That extends to the onyx staircase that winds its way through the magnificent Grand Foyer. The latter provides a centralized area off which many of the ship's public areas are located. The *Infinity* is one of the first ships to feature glass-enclosed elevators offering ocean or Alaskan coastal views.

Unusual areas will also be a hallmark of *Infinity*. The Platinum Club will feature a display of caviar – available for consumption. The Conservatory, located high atop the ship, contains the Magnolia Garden, a combination flower shop and lounge. Of course, the usual things found on a liner of this type are all there, too, such as the Celebrity Theater with Broadway-style shows and the full-service Aqua Spa.

But perhaps what is most special about *Infinity* is its large and excellently designed staterooms. Even the smallest is larger than a mid-grade cabin on most ships. And what can be called the "standard" ocean-view stateroom is definitely a step up from what many cruise passengers will be used to. Besides the extra space (and the likelihood that your stateroom will have a private veranda), all rooms in this class have their own private mini-bar and entertainment center. Enjoy.

⚓ MERCURY *(Celebrity Cruises)*

Built: 1997
Length: 866 feet
Passengers: 1,870
Staterooms: 935
Crew Size: 909
Officers: Greek

Registry: Panama
Gross Tonnage: 77,713
Passenger Decks: 10
Stateroom Size: 172-1,515 sq. ft.
Passenger/Crew Ratio: 2.1:1
Crew: International

MEAL ARRANGEMENTS: There is a spectacular two-level main dining room called the Manhattan Restaurant with early and late seating for all meals. Alternative dining possibilities include buffets in the Palm Springs Café. The Cova Café de Milano offers lighter fare and specialty coffees.

CRUISE STYLE: As with the Infinity, Celebrity Cruises gives the crowd who likes to dress up more opportunity to do so, even in casual Alaska. The Mercury generally features four nights evenly split between formal and informal, while the remaining nights are casual.

PRICE RANGE: All seven-night cruises, regardless of itinerary (Inside Passage or Gulf of Alaska) have the same pricing except for the beginning and end of season positioning cruises, which cost less. The regular stateroom categories begin at $1,699 for the least expensive room and rise to a high of $3,149. Suites begin at $5,629 and reach a maximum of $10,129 for the Penthouse Suite.

All of Celebrity's ships are something special to look at, and *Mercury* is no exception. From the Manhattan Restaurant to the showroom, the interior décor is delightful. Especially worthy of note is the Navigator Club, a two-deck facility with wrap-around windows and seating at different levels that makes this the ideal indoor venue for an Alaskan cruise. The colorful and cheerful décor is highly informal yet the feeling of luxury and elegance is retained. The Navigator becomes a disco during the evening. A feature of Celebrity is the well-known Aqua Spa, considered to be one of the largest and best afloat. The ship also boasts an extensive art collection throughout all of the public areas.

Staterooms are exceptionally spacious and well furnished. They're among the most comfortable of any ship. Little amenities are numerous, even in the lower price categories, and include things like private mini-bar, hair dryer, personal safe and interactive television. There is 24-hour room service. And we should point out that service on board *Mercury* is consistent with the high standards that have been established on all Celebrity line ships.

⚓ NORWEGIAN SKY *(Norwegian Cruise Line)*

Built: 1999
Length: 853 feet
Passengers: 2,002
Staterooms: 1,001
Crew Size: 750
Officers: Norwegian

Registry: Bahamas
Gross Tonnage: 77,104
Passenger Decks: 12
Stateroom Size: 121-489 sq. ft.
Passenger/Crew Ratio: 2.6:1
Crew: European/International

MEAL ARRANGEMENTS: There are three separate dining rooms, each with early and late seatings for all meals, although one of them is a small and intimate facility with all tables seating either two or four persons. In addition, alternative dining choices are extensive. There are two flexible schedule restaurants for dinner, one featuring French/Mediterranean cuisine and the other (called Ciao Chow) boasting Italian and Chinese. There is also a casual café and an outdoor café that are available for breakfast and lunch.

CRUISE STYLE: The Norwegian Sky has one formal night and either one or two informal evenings. The remainder of the cruise is casual.

PRICE RANGE: The seven-day Inside Passage route fares begin at $2,139 and rise to a high of $2,759 in the low season. High season rates are from $2,739 through $3,839. Prices for suites are $3,139 to $5,939 in the low season and from $4,039 to $7,839 during the high season.

The *Norwegian Sky* is a beautiful and graceful new ship that is pleasing to the eye and nicely arranged for easy passenger navigation. The heart of the ship is a striking eight-deck-high atrium. There are even four elevators providing panoramic views. The atrium provides access to all of the ship's public areas which include extensive shopping, a casino, a 1,000-seat showroom with Broadway-style productions, and much more. The ship has an extensive entertainment program, much of which takes place in one of the ship's almost a dozen lounges and bars. One even has a formal afternoon tea service. Among some of the other unique bars are a wine bar and a cigar bar. There's even a small Internet café. The *Norwegian Sky* also boasts excellent programs for small children, as well as teens. The latter even have their own disco. Accommodations are

The Right Cruise For You

25

first-rate, too. Even without getting into the stratosphere high prices of suites, the ship's "standard" deluxe outside cabin is well designed and attractive. However, we do recommend upgrading to at least the third category from the bottom, price-wise. This is because some of the cabins in the lower categories are on the small side.

⚓ NORWEGIAN WIND *(Norwegian Cruise Line)*

Built: 1993	Registry: Bahamas
Length: 623 feet	Gross Tonnage: 39,217
Passengers: 1,246	Passenger Decks: 11
Staterooms: 623	Stateroom Size: 140-350 sq. ft.
Crew Size: 483	Passenger/Crew Ratio: 2.6:1
Officers: Norwegian	Crew: European/International

MEAL ARRANGEMENTS: The ship has early and late seating in the main dining room. The Terraces is a beautiful room seating less than 300 people and a great place to enjoy a meal while the scenery passes by through 20-foot-high floor-to-ceiling windows. You can also opt to dine at Le Bistro, an intimate French-style café that provides elegant surroundings for just 76 patrons. As with most ships you can have an elaborate buffet for both breakfast and lunch.

CRUISE STYLE: There is a single formal evening and either one or two informal evenings. All other nights are a casual style.

PRICE RANGE: The basic cruise fare in the regular stateroom category is from $2,539 through $3,139 while suites go for from $3,439 to $5,439. Value season fares, however, are generally less than half of the so-called brochure price.

The key word in describing this sleek and beautiful vessel is spacious. The public areas (including lounges and theaters) have been designed with open space for everyone in mind. Even the decks are wider than on most other ships. While most of the attractive staterooms also feature plenty of room, those cabins in the lower-priced categories are more similar in size to industry norms. Besides having lots of room in the public areas, these areas are also quite pleasing to the eye. The aforementioned Terraces Dining Room is simply gorgeous and the Stardust Lounge is an excellent showroom. For casual conversation and watching the scenery, the Observatory Lounge is a good choice. Except for a few relatively small staterooms in the lowest price categories, accommodations on the *Norwegian Wind* are first rate in all important aspects – space, design and amenities. Although the passenger/crew ratio of this ship isn't among the best in terms of numbers, we haven't heard of any undue amount of complaints regarding the level of service.

⚓ OCEAN PRINCESS *(Princess Cruises)*

Built: 2000	Registry: Britain
Length: 856 feet	Gross Tonnage: 77,000
Passengers: 1,950	Passenger Decks: 10
Staterooms: 1,011	Stateroom Size: 175 sq. ft. (avg.)
Crew Size: 900	Passenger/Crew Ratio: 2.2:1
Officers: European	Crew: International

MEAL ARRANGEMENTS: There is early and late seatings for all meals in either of the two main dining rooms. The Ocean Princess offers a variety of alternative restaurants. In addition to a regular sit-down meal in a specialty restaurant or casual grill, passengers can choose from a pizzeria, food court and buffet. Dining is available on a 24-hour basis.

CRUISE STYLE: There is one formal night and two informal nights. The remainder are casual. However, cruise-goers who prefer to be casual at all times can do so by avoiding the main dining rooms.

PRICE RANGE: Regular staterooms have a price range of from $1,699 to $3,149 for the eight-day cruise. Suites begin at $4,099 and rise to a maximum of $5,079.

This is one of the three "sister" ships of the *Dawn Princess*, so the description of that ship applies here as well.

⚓ RADIANCE OF THE SEAS
(Royal Caribbean Cruise Line)

Built: 2001
Length: 961 feet
Passengers: 2,001
Staterooms: 1,050
Crew Size: 859
Officers: European

Registry: Liberia
Gross Tonnage: 85,000
Passenger Decks: 12
Stateroom Size: 167-344 sq. ft.;
suites to 1,017 sq. ft.
Passenger/Crew Ratio: 2:4:1
Crew: International

MEAL ARRANGEMENTS: There are early and late seatings for all meals in the main dining room. Several alternative restaurants offer a large choice – from traditional buffets to specialty international restaurants and cafés.

CRUISE STYLE: Indications are that Radiance will be like the other ships in the Royal Caribbean fleet. That is, for week-long cruises there will be a single formal night, one or two informal evenings and the remainder casual.

PRICE RANGE: The prices for the eight-day cruise on this brand-new ship range from $2,049 through $3,279 for regular staterooms and from $3,529 through $7,579 for suites.

RCCL introduces its super-new "vantage class" ship with the February 2001 debut of *Radiance of the Seas*. Since the ship hadn't gone into service prior to press time this description is, necessarily, based on information provided by the cruise line rather than by our preferred method of personal observation and passenger feedback. *Radiance* introduces some new concepts into cruise ship design, including a new generation of quieter engines (not that we've found any of the new cruise ships to be noisy) and higher speeds. It also has several new technologies for protecting the environment. Despite its tremendous size the ship has the overall look and design of a yacht. In keeping with the latest rage in ship design, this vessel features liberal use of glass including floor-to-ceiling glass walls in most public areas and glass elevators facing the sea to whisk passengers between its dozen public decks. More than three-quarters of the outside staterooms have their own private balconies and the pictures we've seen of the spacious units appear to be highly satisfactory in every way. Dining facilities are varied and attractive, but it doesn't appear that *Radiance* breaks any major new ground in this area from other recently deployed Royal Caribbean mega-liners such as *Rhapsody of the Seas* and *Vision of the Seas*.

While *Radiance of the Seas* is definitely going to be adequately described by such superlatives as spectacular, luxurious and gorgeous, the question isn't about how great a ship it is going to be but whether it's great for Alaska cruising in particular. That is, how big is too big for the frequent small port calls of Alaska and the restricted space for cruising some of the more scenic areas? Like many of the largest new ships described in this section, they have already crossed the ideal threshold and it is likely that *Radiance* will have the same problem in the minds of many experienced Alaskan cruise travelers.

⚓ REGAL PRINCESS *(Princess Cruises)*

Built: 1991	Registry: Britain
Length: 811 feet	Gross Tonnage: 70,000
Passengers: 1,590	Passenger Decks: 10
Staterooms: 798	Stateroom Size: 200 sq. ft. (avg.);
Crew Size: 630	suites to 587
Officers: British/Italian	Passenger/Crew Ratio: 2.5:1
	Crew: International

MEAL ARRANGEMENTS: There is one main dining room, which works on an early/late seating basis for all meals. Although the alternative dining options aren't quite as extensive on the Regal Princess as the other ships of this line that are in Alaska, passengers can still choose from a variety of eateries that range from a food court or buffet all the way up to a casual grill.

CRUISE STYLE: There is one formal night and two informal nights. The remainder of the evenings are casual although those who prefer to remain casual all the time can do so by opting for one or more of the alternative dining options.

PRICE RANGE: The eight-day cruise has a price range from $1,699 to $3,139 for regular staterooms and from $3,189 to $4,499 for suites.

Although the *Regal Princess* is considered by the company to be one of their "Grand Class" ships, it is considerably smaller than the other Princess liners in this category. While it has all of the amenities and facilities that people expect from the largest ships, those who find that the biggest mega-liners are just a bit too much for their liking will probably appreciate the *Regal Princess*. Noted architect Renzo Piano designed this ship and it has met with some controversy. The architect envisioned creating a ship based on the graceful silhouette of a dolphin and the rounded corners do, indeed, evoke some comparison to the shape of a dolphin. While we like the overall appearance, especially the large enclosed forward section of the Sun Deck, we must also point out that a number of ship industry raters and critics have had bad things to say about the way this ship looks.

Well, most of the time you'll be on the ship, not looking at it, so the exterior appearance may not be all that important to you in the first place. The ship has a spacious and well thought out interior design with most of the public facilities placed on the beautiful Promenade Deck. There are plenty of facilities for recreation that include a pool with a swim-up bar à la Caribbean or Las Vegas. The extensive use of rich teak wood and lots of shiny brass give the ship an elegant feel, which is further enhanced by an almost museum-like art collection. Stateroom layout and design are first-rate.

⚓ RHAPSODY OF THE SEAS
(Royal Caribbean Cruise Line)

Built: 1997
Length: 915 feet
Passengers: 2,000
Staterooms: 1,000
Crew Size: 784
Officers: Norwegian

Registry: Norway
Gross Tonnage: 78,491
Passenger Decks: 10
Stateroom Size: From 148 sq. ft.; suites to 1,509
Passenger/Crew Ratio: 2.6:1
Crew: International

MEAL ARRANGEMENTS: Early and late seatings for all meals in the main dining room. Although the Edelweiss Dining Room is a beautiful sight, and the food and service are excellent, the capacity of 1,179 people per seating is a negative aspect for some. However, there are a good number of alternative dining choices. The Windjammer Café essentially offers the same cuisine as in the main restaurant but in a much more casual atmosphere.

CRUISE STYLE: The Rhapsody cruise experience will require formal attire on one evening and informal on either one or two additional evenings. The remainder of the cruise will be casual dress.

PRICE RANGE: Regular stateroom prices begin at $1,949 and rise to a high of $3,179. The price for suites begins at $3,429 with a high of $7,679.

This ship was the second in a series of RCCL ships that, in some ways, brought a new standard of size and luxury to the cruise world. The ship is huge, as the statistics indicate, but there is a feeling of space. Perhaps part of the reason for that feeling is the extensive use of glass. Entire walls are made of glass and it almost always seems that you're actually out on the open seas while aboard. This provides great viewing from mostpublic areas and even extends to the large and well-equipped gym. The latter is on the sports-and view-oriented Compass Deck, which features a large retractable canopy. If you're lucky enough to have good weather while in Alaska, the canopy might well be open. In keeping with an increasingly popular theme on cruise ships, *Rhapsody* has an excellent art collection. You'll encounter paintings in just about every nook and cranny of the ship. The extensive public areas will dazzle you from top to bottom and from bow to stern but we are especially fond of the stunning décor of the Broadway Melodies Theater. The ship boasts separate programs and areas for teens and younger children.

Large staterooms are a hallmark of this class of ship. The most common type of cabin has 153 square feet, generous for many ships. Moreover, it is nicely decorated and well equipped. The colorful curtains add an informal touch of home and are also used to separate the sleeping area from the living area. The majority of rooms (except in the lowest price categories) have a private balcony.

⚓ RYNDAM (Holland America)

Built: 1994
Length: 720 feet
Passengers: 1,266
Staterooms: 633
Crew Size: 602
Officers: Dutch/European

Registry: Netherlands
Gross Tonnage: 55,451
Passenger Decks: 10
Stateroom Size: 182-225 sq. ft.;
suites to 563
Passenger/Crew Ratio: 2.1:1
Crew: Indonesian/Filipino

MEAL ARRANGEMENTS: The main dining room has open seating for breakfast and lunch but early and late seatings for dinner. Alternative dining options include the Lido buffet for breakfast and lunch. On most evenings the Lido is available for sit-down dinners. The Terrace Grill offers casual alfresco style for favorites such as burgers, pasta and even tacos.

CRUISE STYLE: There is one formal night and two informal evenings. The remainder of the cruise is casual.

PRICE RANGE: Fares for the eight-day cruise range from a low of $1,163 to $2,727 for regular staterooms and from $3,163 to $8,087 for suites during the low season. The tariff increases progressively to the highest rates of $1,963 to $3,527 for regular staterooms and $4,363-$9,020 for suites during the high season.

Most Holland America line ships aren't, at least from an exterior point of view, of the same "drop-dead gorgeous" variety of many of the other newer mega-liners. Perhaps it is their dark bottom hulls and generally unimaginative shape. This is true for the *Ryndam* and its two sister ships. However, the interiors are beautifully designed and exude the luxury that is expected from a cruise experience. Public areas display a generous use of teak wood, many works of art, and beautiful fresh flowers. Interior architectural highlights include a multi-story atrium, a two-story main dining room, and a two-tiered showroom. A great place to watch the passing scenery is high up in the Crow's Nest Lounge, where you'll be surrounded on three sides by large glass windows. In addition to the usual recreational facilities, one of this ship's swimming pools features a retractable dome so that the outside weather won't interfere with your swimming plans. All of the staterooms feature easy-on-the-eyes pastel tones and comfortable, tasteful furnishings. Upper-priced suites are the epitome of luxury.

Holland America is known for outstanding service, and the *Ryndam* class of ships won't disappoint you in that regard. On-board services and activities include the University at Sea program, Club Hal for children ages five through 17 and an Internet café. The ship's spa features a Steiner of London program. In addition to the on-board Alaskan naturalist expert, all Holland America Alaskan sailings now feature a Native Artists-in-Residence Program. You can watch while craftspeople sculpt, paint, weave or demonstrate a variety of other skills.

⚓ SEA PRINCESS *(Princess Cruises)*

Built: 1998	Registry: Britain
Length: 856 feet	Gross Tonnage: 77,000
Passengers: 1,950	Passenger Decks: 10
Staterooms: 1,011	Stateroom Size: 175 sq. ft.(avg.)
Crew Size: 900	Passenger/Crew Ratio: 2.2:1
Officers: European	Crew: International

MEAL ARRANGEMENTS: There is early and late seating for all meals in either of the two main dining rooms. Optional dining choices are available on a 24-hour basis. These include a specialty restaurant, grill, food court, pizzeria and buffet.

CRUISE STYLE: There is one formal night and two informal nights. The remainder are casual. However, you can go casual all the time if you always choose to have dinner in one of the alternative restaurants.

PRICE RANGE: The eight-day cruise has a price tag of $1,699 to $3,149 for regular staterooms and from $4,099 to $5,079 for suites.

This is one of the three "sister" ships of the *Dawn Princess*, so the description for that ship also applies to this one.

⚓ SEVEN SEAS MARINER *(Radisson Seven Seas)*

Built: 2001
Length: 670 feet
Passengers: 708
Staterooms: 354
Crew Size: 445
Officers: European

Registry: France
Gross Tonnage: 50,000
Passenger Decks: 8
Stateroom Size: 301-1,580 sq. ft.
(with balcony)
Passenger/Crew Ratio: 1.6:1
Crew: French/European

MEAL ARRANGEMENTS: The Seven Seas allows its passengers to choose from one of four different restaurants. All of them offer the convenience and ambiance of single seating. Unlike other cruise ships it does not have a main dining room in the traditional sense. Complimentary wine is included at dinner. One restaurant, Signature, even boasts a world-famous French chef.

CRUISE STYLE: The Captain's dinner is the lone formal night. Dress at all other times depends upon the restaurant chosen rather than individual nights being designated for specific dress. You could, in theory, go casual every night. However, this could well be the most sophisticated ship cruising to Alaska, so the casual traveler is likely to be the exception rather than the rule.

PRICE RANGE: The eight-day Seward to Vancouver cruise fare begins at $2,495 and rises to $10,395 for the most luxurious accommodations, while a round trip from Vancouver for the same period of time ranges from $2,695 to $11,695. There are also some 10- and 12-day trips that begin at $3,095 and have a maximum price of $18,695.

By today's standards, the *Seven Seas Mariner* almost qualifies as a "small ship" when compared to most of the newer mega-liners. However, we include it here because the facilities and style of the cruise are definitely in keeping with the "large ship" crowd. This luxurious floating palace made its inaugural cruise in the spring of 2001 so it is one of the newest ships offering Alaska cruises. Moreover, it brings a new standard of luxury to cruising in general because it is an all-suite ship and every stateroom has its own private balcony. Even the smallest stateroom (252 square feet without the balcony) is very generous for a cruise ship. There are several categories of accommodations to choose from, with the best being akin to a nice size house. The *Seven Seas Mariner* has the highest space-per-guest ratio in the cruise industry. On-board facilities and activities compare favorably with much larger ships and there is even a full-service spa. The décor is exquisite in a refined and tasteful manner. The level of luxury here is definitely a notch above the industry standard but, alas, as you can see from the price information, you do pay for it! The *Seven Seas Mariner* has a no-tipping policy.

⚓ STATENDAM *(Holland America)*

Built: 1993
Length: 720 feet
Passengers: 1,266
Staterooms: 633
Crew Size: 602
Officers: Dutch/European

Registry: Netherlands
Gross Tonnage: 55,451
Passenger Decks: 10
Stateroom Size: 182-225 sq. ft.; suites to 563
Passenger/Crew Ratio: 2.1:1
Crew: Indonesian/Filipino

MEAL ARRANGEMENTS: There is open seating in the main dining room for breakfast and lunch but early and late seatings for dinner. Like its sister ships, the Statendam offers a choice of alternative dining for those who don't wish a formal sit-down affair. A breakfast and lunch buffet is available at the Lido and it also has a good dinner menu except on the ship's formal evening. Fast-food type fare can be had at the Terrace Grill.

CRUISE STYLE: There is one formal evening during the cruise and two informal nights. The remainder of the evenings are casual.

PRICE RANGE: Fares for the eight-day cruise range from a low of $1,163 to $2,727 for regular staterooms and from $3,163-$8,087 for suites during the low season. The tariff increases progressively to the highest rates of $1,963 to $3,527 for regular staterooms and $4,363-$9,020 for suites during the high season. These prices are for the Glacier Discovery itinerary (Vancouver/Seward). Fares for the Inside Passage itinerary are within $25 in all categories.

The *Statendam* is one of a series of sister ships operated by Holland America. See the description under the *Ryndam* for further details on ship design, facilities and activities.

⚓ SUN PRINCESS *(Princess Cruises)*

Built: 1995	Registry: Britain
Length: 856 feet	Gross Tonnage: 77,000
Passengers: 1,950	Passenger Decks: 10
Staterooms: 1,011	Stateroom Size: 175 sq. ft. (avg.)
Passenger/Crew Ratio: 2.2:1	Crew Size: 900
Officers: European	Crew: International

MEAL ARRANGEMENTS: There is early and late seating for all meals in either of the two main dining rooms. Optional dining choices are available on a 24-hour basis. These include specialty restaurant, grill, food court, pizzeria and buffet.

CRUISE STYLE: There is one formal night and two informal nights. The remainder are casual. However, you can go casual all the time if you always choose to have dinner in one of the alternative restaurants.

PRICE RANGE: The eight-day cruise has a price tag of $1,699 to $3,149 for regular staterooms and from $4,099 to $5,079 for suites.

The *Sun Princess* was the first of Princess' new breed of megaliners. It has since been joined by its three sisters, the *Dawn Princess*, *Ocean Princess* and *Sea Princess*. See the listing for the *Dawn Princess* for further descriptive details.

⚓ VEENDAM *(Holland America)*

Built: 1996	Registry: Bahamas
Length: 720 feet	Gross Tonnage: 55,451
Passengers: 1,266	Passenger Decks: 10
Staterooms: 633	Stateroom Size: 182-225 sq. ft.
Crew Size: 602	Passenger/Crew Ratio: 2.1:1
Officers: Dutch/European	Crew: Indonesian/Filipino

MEAL ARRANGEMENTS: There is open seating in the main dining room for breakfast and lunch but early and late seating for dinner. Besides the main dining room, passengers may opt for the Lido Restaurant (buffet-style for breakfast and lunch and menu at dinner time). However, the Lido is closed on the evening of the Captain's dinner. Children and other "nosh" style eaters will like the alfresco Terrace Grill's selection of hamburgers, tacos and pasta.

CRUISE STYLE: There is one formal evening and two informal evenings during the cruise. The remainder of the nights are all casual.

PRICE RANGE: Fares for the eight-day cruise range from a low of $1,163 to $2,727 for regular staterooms and from $3,163-$8,087 for suites during the low season. The tariff increases progressively to the highest rates of $1,963 to $3,527 for regular staterooms and $4,363-$9,020 for suites during the high season. These prices are for the Glacier Discovery itinerary (Vancouver/Seward). Fares for the Inside Passage itinerary are within $25 in all categories.

A sister of both the *Ryndam* and *Statendam*, refer to the listing for the *Ryndam* for further descriptive details on this ship's design, facilities and activities.

⚓ VISION OF THE SEAS
(Royal Caribbean Cruise Line)

Built: 1998	Registry: Liberia
Length: 915 feet	Gross Tonnage: 78,491
Passengers: 2,000	Passenger Decks: 10
Staterooms: 1,000	Stateroom Size: 149-1,059 sq. ft.
Crew Size: 765	Passenger/Crew Ratio: 2.6:1
Officers: International	Crew: International

MEAL ARRANGEMENTS: There is one dining room with early and late seatings for all meals. Like its counterpart, Rhapsody of the Seas, the main dining room is beautiful but the nearly 1,200-persons per seating may be a bit of a turn-off for some people. In that case, go for one of the alternative dining options, including the usual buffet or the Windjammer Café with its more gourmet style of food and casual service.

CRUISE STYLE: Vision's suggested dress code for their week-long voyages is formal attire on one evening and informal on an additional two evenings. The remainder of the cruise will be of a casual nature.

PRICE RANGE: Brochure prices for the eight day cruise begin at $2,049 and rise to a high of $3,279 for regular staterooms. Suite prices range from $3,529 through $7,779.

The Right Cruise For You

Vision of the Seas is among Royal Caribbean's new breed of mega-liner but, as it is the sister of *Rhapsody of the Seas*, you can read the listing of that ship for complete details.

⚓ VOLENDAM *(Holland America)*

Built: 1999
Length: 780 feet
Passengers: 1,440
Staterooms: 720
Crew Size: 647
Officers: Dutch/European

Registry: Netherlands
Gross Tonnage: 63,000
Passenger Decks: 10
Stateroom Size: 182-197 sq. ft.;
suites to 1,216
Passenger/Crew Ratio: 2.2:1
Crew: Indonesian/Filipino

MEAL ARRANGEMENTS: There is open seating in the main dining room for breakfast and lunch but early and late seatings for dinner. While the Volendam has the usual alternative dining options available on all other Holland America ships (i.e., the Lido buffet and dinner restaurant; Terrace Grill for a quick bite), it also has the small and intimate Marco Polo specialty restaurant. The latter is open most evenings.

CRUISE STYLE: The Volendam features a single formal night along with two informal nights. The remainder of the evenings are casual.

PRICE RANGE: The eight-day cruise has fares beginning at $1,173, rising to $2,543 for regular staterooms and from $3,153-$8,090 for suites during the low season. Depending upon departure date these fares rise to a maximum of $1,973-$3,343 for regular staterooms and from $4,553-$9,223 for suites.

This ship, along with the *Zaandam*, represents the newest and best in Holland America's fleet. Again, as in the case of the three sister ships previously described (*Ryndam, Statendam and Veendam*), the *Volendam* is more stately and traditional looking than most of the newer ships in the Alaskan market or elsewhere for that matter. That, no doubt, will appeal to many cruiser lovers. The ship's interior is superb. It is well laid out with spacious decks and public spaces. Many of the public areas are located off the beautiful three-story high central atrium. Multi-level architecture is a trait of this ship; you will find two levels in both the main dining room and in the showroom. The tastefully designed staterooms and suites feature shades of beige and taupe and are generously sized, even in the lower-priced categories. The ship has a huge array of recreational facilities including a swimming pool with a retractable dome and practice tennis courts. Holland America offers a wealth of on-board programs. Some of the general ones are University at Sea and Club Hal for children ages five through 17. The traditional Dutch high tea service is alive and well on these new ships, but they also have new millennium- style facilities such as an Internet café. The spa (Steiner of London) program is one of the most extensive on the high seas.

The *Volendam* cruise experience to Alaska won't let you forget where you are either. They always have a naturalist/Alaska expert on board and now have the added attraction of the Native Artists-in-Residence Program. This will enable you to observe skilled craftspeople as they sculpt or paint or create other types of works of art.

⚓ WESTERDAM *(Holland America)*

Built: 1986; refurbished 1990	Registry: Netherlands
Length: 798 feet	Gross Tonnage: 53,872
Passengers: 1,494	Passenger Decks: 9
Staterooms: 747	Stateroom Size: 131-236 sq. ft.;
Crew Size: 642	suites are 414
Officers: Dutch/European	Passenger/Crew Ratio: 2.3:1
	Crew: Indonesian/Filipino

MEAL ARRANGEMENTS: The main dining room has open seating for breakfast and lunch but early and late seatings for dinner. Other dining options include the Lido (buffet breakfast and lunch; sit-down menu for dinner on all evenings except the Captain's dinner night) and the fast-food style Terrace Grill.

CRUISE STYLE: There is a single formal evening and two informal evenings. The remainder of the cruise is informal.

PRICE RANGE: The eight-day cruise fare begins at $1,153 and rises to $3,223 for regular staterooms while suites go for $4,623. These fares pro-

The Right Cruise For You

gressively rise according to departure date to a maximum of $1,853-$4,090 for regular staterooms and to $5,690 for suites.

As recently as a couple of years ago it was common to see many ships in Alaska that dated from the 1980s. With the debut of so many ships over the past several years, however, the *Westerdam* can be considered to be one of the "grand old dames" of the Alaskan seas. This isn't meant as a criticism, for this fine ship has many excellent attributes that will be of interest to the traditional cruise passenger. The *Westerdam* was, in many ways, the prototype for the newer Holland America ships in Alaska so you can expect the same thoughtful attention to the layout and design of the beautiful public areas. There are plenty of lounges and great viewing areas both inside and out on the teak decks. The range of activities is virtually the same as on the other ships of this line and includes the Native Artists-in-Residence Program and the excellent children/teens program called Club Hal. The level of service on the *Westerdam* is extremely high. If we have one complaint it is that the staterooms are not as large as on the other Holland-America ships. It is, therefore, probably wiser to upgrade to a better class of accommodation on this ship than on other vessels of the same line.

⚓ ZAANDAM *(Holland America)*

Built: 2000
Length: 780 feet
Passengers: 1,440
Staterooms: 720
Crew Size: 647
Officers: Dutch/European

Registry: Netherlands
Gross Tonnage: 63,000
Passenger Decks: 10
Stateroom Size: 182-197 sq. ft.;
suites to 1,216
Passenger/Crew Ratio: 2.2:1
Crew: Indonesian/Filipino

MEAL ARRANGEMENTS: The main dining room has open seating for breakfast and lunch but early/late seatings for dinner. Along with the Volendam, this ship has the most alternative dining options of any Holland America ship in Alaska. As they are exactly the same as its sister ship, the Volendam, see that listing for more details.

CRUISE STYLE: There is one formal evening and two informal evenings on all Zaandam cruises. The remainder of the trip is casual.

PRICE RANGE: The eight-day cruise has fares beginning at $1,173, rising to $2,543 for regular staterooms and from $3,153-$8,090 for suites during the low season. Depending upon departure date these fares rise to a maximum of $1,973-$3,343 for regular staterooms and from $4,553-$9,223 for suites.

It's been a long time since there hasn't been a Holland America ship called the *Nieuw Amsterdam* sailing to Alaska, but for the year 2001 that well recognized name is out and the newer and more luxurious *Zaandam* is in. *Zaandam* is the sister ship of the *Volendam* and all of the necessary details can be found under the listing for that ship.

⚓ How to Choose a Stateroom

That completes the big ship inventory. Once you've decided which ship to book, you'll have to choose what type of stateroom you want. This is the primary cost determinant and the price range is considerable. The best are generally more than twice as expensive as the lowest-priced room category.

Two important factors to consider when selecting a room category are size and location. The bigger the room the higher the price, with the top categories usually being suites. One has to wonder if the biggest is really worth the money, especially considering that you probably won't be spending that much time inside. On the other hand, we're not dealing with hotel-sized rooms here, so you probably won't want the smallest room either, especially if you are claustrophobic. Be sure you know what you're getting when you reserve.

For comparison purposes, keep in mind that even an average-sized motel room measuring 12' x 24' would contain 288 square feet. That's quite a bit larger than the standard room on even the best ships.

Regarding location, you'll find that the more modern ships (as well as the smaller ones) usually have the majority of their rooms located on the outside. It's nice to wake up to beautiful scenery passing by your window each morning. But if you're not squeamish about sleeping in a windowless room, an inside stateroom can save some money and might do just as well from a comfort standpoint. The middle section of any ship tends to give the smoothest ride but, again, this is rarely a problem on cruises to Alaska – you won't run into any tropical hurricanes. The key to finding the location you want is simple: just study the deck plans in the cruise brochures.

Small Ships

Make a conscious effort not to compare these ships to the larger cruise liners. They are not in the same category, which means you're comparing apples and oranges. Except for the *Universe Explorer* we'll depart from the usual statistical listings and rely on narrative descriptions to familiarize you with these vessels.

⚓ CLIPPER ODYSSEY *(Clipper Cruises)*

PRICE RANGE: $5,320-7,400 for an 11-day cruise and from $6,510-$8,780 for a 14-day cruise. Suites are, respectively $7,320 and $9,280. The 14-day excursion includes airfare from Anchorage on the Asia/Pacific segment of the trip.

This Dutch-designed and Japanese-built ship was launched in 1989. It is 340 feet long (making it fairly big for this category of ship) and carries a maximum of 128 passengers in 64 all-outside staterooms and suites. The average stateroom size is 186 square feet, which is quite spacious for a small ship. Upgraded accommodations include tub baths and separate sitting areas. The dining room can accommodate all passengers in a single seating. There is a swimming pool on board, something most small ships don't have, although it's not all that likely that you will have the opportunity to make use of it in Alaska. The ship is equipped with Zodiac rafts for more in-depth exploration. The *Clipper Odyssey* has a cruising speed of 14 knots. That is also faster than most other small ships but still considerably slower than the big cruise liners. But then again, going slow in Alaskan waters isn't necessarily a negative unless you're in a big rush to see the scenery pass you by.

⚓ EXECUTIVE EXPLORER
(Glacier Bay Tours & Cruises)

PRICE RANGE: Prices begin at $2,780 for an eight-day cruise.

The *Executive Explorer* is even smaller and more intimate than most of the other small ships of this company. Carrying a maximum of 49 passengers in 25 all outside staterooms with large view windows, the 99-foot long vessel features a large video library where you can learn more about Alaska (each cabin has its own VCR). The crew is all American as are the other ships of this line. The interesting high profile of this ship allows for elevated viewing of the scenery.

⚓ SEA LION & SEA BIRD *(Linblad Expeditions)*

PRICE RANGE: Fares range from $3,690 to $5,350 for an eight-day cruise.

These two American-built-and-registered sister vessels were launched in 1981 and 1982 and can each accommodate a maximum of 70 passengers in 37 cabins. The four-deck ships measure 152 feet in length and carry several kayaks and Zodiac landing craft for special excursions. All of the cabins are outside and are fairly spacious and quite attractive. Public facilities consist of a dining room, observation lounge and sun deck. The lounge is the focal point for most ship activities, including a daily "recap" of the day's events that allows passengers to ask questions of the staff.

⚓ UNIVERSE EXPLORER *(World Explorer Cruises)*

Built: 1957; refurbished 1995	Registry: Panama
Length: 617 feet	Tonnage: 23,500
Passengers: 740	Passenger Decks: 8
Staterooms: 371	Staterooms size: 104-293 sq. ft.
Crew Size: 365	Passenger/Crew Ratio: 2.0:1
Officers: American/European	Crew: American/International

MEAL ARRANGEMENTS: The Hamilton Dining Room seats 375 people, which almost puts it in the "intimate" category compared to some of the larger ships. There are early and late seatings for all meals. A buffet-style breakfast or lunch is available in the Harbour Grill. If the weather permits, the Universe Explorer also devotes one evening to an on-deck barbecue!.

CRUISE STYLE: This ship has a more casual atmosphere than any of the larger ships. In fact, although two nights are considered "formal" by World Explorer Cruises, they are, in fact, equivalent to the "informal" category by our standards. The remainder of the evenings are all casual.

PRICE RANGE: $1,497-$3,995 for a 15-day cruise. These prices include all port charges. In addition, World Explorer Cruises has relatively low rates for single supplements and has more than their share of money-saving rates on an already well-priced package.

The *Universe Explorer* is larger than the other "small ships" in this section but smaller than any of the major cruise liners now sailing to Alaska. By comparison, only the all-suite *Seven Seas Mariner* carries fewer passengers (708) and only two of the "large" category ships are under 700 feet in length (but are both longer than the *Universe Explorer*). However, we include the *Universe Explorer* here not only due to size considerations but also because of the nature of their cruise experience. As you will see when you read about the various ship itineraries, this ship provides an in-depth experience that is much more akin to the personalized small ship cruises. A traditional looking ship (and one of only a couple of American-built vessels of its size still in service), the *Universe Explorer* can no longer compete on looks with the mega-liners but it is, especially since the recent refurbishing, an attractive and very comfortable vessel. The exterior has been repainted entirely in white. Public areas and facilities are similar to those found on the major cruise lines but they're smaller and far less elaborate. We especially like the circular Mid Ocean Lounge, which provides excellent viewing conditions and is also the focal point for many on-board Alaska-related programs. The ship has the largest library afloat and an Internet café.

⚓ WILDERNESS ADVENTURER
(Glacier Bay Tours & Cruises)

PRICE RANGE: Prices begin at $2,190 for an eight-day cruise.

A recent major renovation of this already nice small ship (72 passengers) has increased creature comforts in the form of new furnishings and a revamped dining room. Improved aesthetics are also in evidence. Measuring 157 feet in length, the *Wilderness Adventurer* is uniquely designed for the "soft" adventure travel of its name. The ship is equipped with kayaks and Zodiac craft. Its size and design allow the ship to be brought practically onto the shore so passengers can literally walk off the boat and onto land.

⚓ WILDERNESS DISCOVERER
(Glacier Bay Tours & Cruises)

PRICE RANGE: Prices begin at $2,295 for an eight-day cruise.

The *Wilderness Discoverer* carries a maximum of 88 passengers in 42 comfortable outside staterooms. The 169-foot long vessel is a low and sleek-looking vessel that will likely remind many passengers of a luxury yacht. The three-deck vessel fea-

The Right Cruise For You

tures, in addition to its dining room, a lounge and several outside viewing areas. This is typical of all ships in this class.

⚓ WILDERNESS EXPLORER
(Glacier Bay Tours & Cruises)

PRICE RANGE: Prices begin at $1,680 for a seven-day cruise.

This 112-foot-long small ship is a soft-adventure traveler's delight. Privacy is the name of the game as the ship can only accommodate 34 passengers in 17 nicely decorated staterooms. The knowledgeable American crew will take you on a slow-paced adventure through the 49th state as the *Wilderness Explorer* can only travel at a speed of nine knots per hour. The exterior profile of the ship isn't one of the more attractive small ships but you shouldn't let that deter you. In fact, the design is deliberate – looking something like an upgraded trawler, the *Wilderness Explorer* is specially designed for scenic cruising and easy access into the ship's kayaks and Zodiac rafts.

⚓ YORKTOWN CLIPPER *(Clipper Cruises)*

PRICE RANGE: $3,560-$5,470 for a 13-day cruise; $3,260-$5,010 for a 12-day cruise; and $2,310-$3,550 for an eight-day cruise.

The 138-passenger *Yorktown Clipper* was built in 1988 and has 69 all-outside cabins. The 257-foot long vessel boasts a yacht-like atmosphere and a friendly feeling on board. Yet, the staterooms are on a par with many of the biggest and best ships both in size and décor. The spacious observation lounge provides excellent viewing conditions and is where many lectures and other cruise-related activities take place.

Alaska Marine Highway Ferries

The various ferries on each of the Marine Highway System's routes cannot be compared to either the large cruise ships or the smaller ones. In size, they generally fall somewhere in between the other two. The AMH has a total of nine ships built between 1963 and 1996. The smallest is 193 feet long, while the biggest measures 408 feet. Passenger capacity ranges from 190 to 625. A few that run on the shortest routes don't have any staterooms, while the one with the most cabins has 108 (not all with private bath).

These ships were designed primarily as a means of transportation, and not for pleasure cruising. Therefore, they lack almost all of the luxury amenities associated with cruising. Onboard dining is simple and adequate, but not a gourmet experience. Much space on each ferry is devoted to carrying vehicles, so you won't find lots in the way of shopping or recreational facilities. Staterooms are also on the simple side and, for most people, will do nicely for a night or two, but might become a little too Spartan feeling after a week or more of port-hopping. A lot of students and other free spirits (i.e., people without the money to afford passage on a cruise ship) opt to take "deck space" on the ferries. This means they camp out with their sleeping bags in whatever comfortable spot they can find. We aren't fancy travelers, but this idea doesn't do much for our sense of vacation aesthetics.

Unlike cruises, everything on a ferry is à la carte – you pay for passage (rates dependent upon accommodation classification) and anything else is extra. All ferries have a naturalist on board to narrate during passage through especially interesting or scenic areas and to answer questions.

The Right Cruise For You

Fares can range from as low as $20 to several hundred per run, depending upon length and level of accommodations. An Alaska Pass good for unlimited travel in an eight- or 15-day period is also available. Prices are, respectively, about $500 and $750.

Although there is a degree of flexibility in traveling by ferry, it's not as open-ended as you might think. You have to be able to adapt your itinerary to meet their limited fixed schedule. It was possible in the past to just show up before sailing time, buy a ticket and hop on board, but because of the increasing popularity of Alaska travel, that has been stopped. You should have reservations and tickets in hand prior to each leg of your journey. For further information on the Alaska Marine Highway's routes, see pages 66-68.

Gateway Cities & Getting to Your Ship

Almost any cruise that you book will include air transportation to the embarkation city. In the case of the larger cruise lines this is most often Vancouver, Canada. However, beginning in 2000 a couple of cruise lines began offering departures from Seattle and it appears that this will be an increasingly available option as time goes by. The advantage of Seattle is that there are better air connections into that location than there are to Vancouver (unless you live in Canada). Both cities have modern cruise ship terminals that are in the heart of the city, which makes getting to your embarkation point easy if you choose to spend some time there. In both cases it is a good ride from the airport. However, transportation is usually provided by the cruise line. There are some Alaska cruises that depart (or return) from as far away as San Francisco or Los Angeles. We don't usually recommend these because you spend a lot of time getting to or from Alaska. However, if you are looking for a cruise experience, you might want to consider these options as well.

Although a package deal usually provides a good price on the air portion of your journey, it is sometimes possible to do better on your own. Arranging the trip yourself affords you more flexibility in regard to flight times, rather than one that has been mass-booked by the cruise line. If traveling to Vancouver on your own you might want to check out the schedules for Air Canada or United Airlines, who offer extensive flights. Often, you will be booked onto a flight to Seattle and then bused to Vancouver. The ride takes about three hours and traverses pleasant scenery. Many airlines have service into Seattle, including Continental, United, AmericaWest and Northwest, as well as Alaska Airlines. Several lower cost airlines, including Southwest, also serve Seattle.

The small ship operators will also book your flight, although the same considerations apply. If booking on your own, you'll have to make connections into smaller airports such as Juneau. Making your own reservations (without the cruise line's help) becomes a necessity if you're using the Alaska Marine Highway System to get from one place to another. If you plan to travel on the AMH, the best bet is to use Alaska Airlines, which offers direct flights from many US cities. Within Alaska they serve Anchorage, Fairbanks, Juneau, Ketchikan and other destinations.

Ship Itineraries

Now that you're ready to step aboard just about any ship, it's time to burst the bubble a little bit and tell you why some cruises just aren't as good as others. When it comes to Alaska cruising, bigger isn't always better. Many of the ports have very limited docking facilities, which means that large ships often cannot dock at all – anchor is dropped in the harbor and

The Right Cruise For You

you are shuttled into town via the ship's launches (now more commonly called tenders), small vessels that accommodate about a hundred people.

Admittedly, it can be fun and even exciting to board the tender and motor into port one or two times during a cruise. But a daily routine of battling long lines to get onto a tender can wear thin quickly. After a few times it's more of a time-consuming nuisance than a pleasure. Having the ship tie up at the dock certainly gives you more time to explore the attractions ashore. Also, for the elderly or anyone who has a physical handicap, the tender can be a much more difficult way to get into port. This doesn't mean it can't be done by older persons – they do it all the time; it's just another consideration.

A second and even more important limitation faced by the largest of the ships is that of navigating smaller channels of water. They cannot use some of the narrow and very scenic waterways that the smaller vessels are able to reach. Thus, their itineraries are forced to exclude some worthwhile sights (which they won't mention to you). Also, because of the larger turning space they need, some of the more behemoth-sized new ships cannot get as close to the face of the spectacular glaciers. And there is nothing quite like nudging up to a towering wall of ice known as a tidal glacier!

This doesn't mean that every cruise liner has some or all of these limitations. While we won't say there's a specific cut-off point, a ship that measures about 650 feet long or under can be considered to be in the "small" category.

Itineraries on the cruise liners take one of two basic forms. The first is an Inside Passage trip that begins and ends in Vancouver. It hits most of the ports between Ketchikan and Skagway as well as the scenic attractions along the waterway, usually including Glacier Bay National Park. The other type goes under various names but departs from Vancouver, sails the Inside

Passage and then goes on to the Gulf of Alaska before ending in Seward. You are then transported via land the approximately 130 miles between Seward and Anchorage. Of course, half of the itineraries on these cruises operate in reverse, that is, from Anchorage to Vancouver. A few of the larger cruise ships used to sail all the way to Anchorage, but this is no longer the case, so remember when reviewing the itineraries that those beginning or ending in Anchorage actually do so in Seward with transfer to Anchorage by bus. Also completely gone from the scene (at least for now) in the big ship category are the Gulf of Alaska excursions that ended in Whittier, where passengers used to hop a scenic train ride on into Anchorage. The small ships can follow either of the main two patterns but most (especially the really small ships) concentrate on the Inside Passage.

Individual ship itineraries will be discussed below in alphabetical sequence, with the exception of ships from the same line with identical itineraries, which are grouped together. An evaluation of each itinerary is given.

The itineraries here give the "regular" schedule for each ship. That is, the one they follow most of the time. It's common for a ship to have a different itinerary for its first Alaskan voyage of the season as well as the last. Often this means that instead of Vancouver, the southern terminus for the voyage will be San Francisco or other West Coast port. A couple might even go from Seward into an Asian port. These "once a season" itineraries (called repositioning cruises) are not mentioned here but you can inquire with the individual cruise lines as to their availability. However, if a ship usually splits its voyages between two or more itineraries, this will be noted.

The Right Cruise For You

Large Cruise Liners

⚓ CARNIVAL SPIRIT

Offers two choices of seven-day cruises. One is the "Glacier Route" from Vancouver to Seward (or the reverse). The other is the round-trip "Glacier Bay" from Vancouver.

ITINERARY: The Glacier Route covers the Inside Passage and the Gulf of Alaska (northbound and southbound itineraries vary a bit). Both cruise the Inside Passage and College Fjord and stop at Ketchikan, Juneau and Skagway. The northbound trip also stops at Sitka and cruises the Endicott Arm and College Fjord. On the southbound itinerary, the port call is Valdez with scenic cruising of Yakutat Bay and Hubbard Glacier. The Glacier Bay itinerary sails the Inside Passage and Glacier Bay with ports of call at Juneau, Skagway and Ketchikan.

EVALUATION: Both itineraries are quite similar to what we would term the "standard" Inside Passage and Gulf of Alaska routes. The only major item missed on the Glacier Route is Glacier Bay, but that is not uncommon these days among the larger ships. The southbound itinerary is somewhat better because Yakutat Bay and Hubbard Glacier are superior to the Endicott Arm by a fairly wide margin. Valdez is in a prettier setting than Sitka although the latter town will be of more interest to those who seek Alaskan history. The Glacier Bay itinerary has no major faults but doesn't break any significant new ground, either. For a big ship you can't find too much to complain about in these itineraries.

⚓ CRYSTAL HARMONY

Offering a 12-day Inside Passage cruise departing from and returning to San Francisco.

ITINERARY: Ketchikan, Juneau, Glacier Bay, Sitka, Skagway, cruising the Inside Passage, Vancouver and Victoria.

EVALUATION: As an Inside Passage-only cruise, the itinerary is generally of average quality. It does hit all of the most important spots. The best aspect of the ship's itinerary is that all departures do sail through Glacier Bay National Park. However, a problem from our point of view is the round-trip from San Francisco. More than two full days are spent getting to and from that city, which is fine if you just want to cruise. But what appears at first glance to be a 12-day Alaska cruise is actually six days. Vancouver and Victoria are both worthwhile places to visit but the time doing so could be better spent pre- or post-cruise rather than as a one-day port call in each case. Whether or not this is the right itinerary for you comes down to a question of how many nights you want to cruise. If the cruise experience is quite important to you, then you may find that the time to and from San Francisco could be a plus. Just be aware that this is not a 12-day Alaskan trip.

⚓ DAWN PRINCESS

This ship offers a seven-day Gulf of Alaska cruise from Vancouver to Seward, or the reverse itinerary.

ITINERARY: Cruising the Inside Passage, College Fjord and either Glacier Bay or Hubbard Glacier. Port calls are Ketchikan, Juneau and Skagway. Northbound and southbound itineraries do not differ.

EVALUATION: Princess calls this itinerary their "Voyage of the Glaciers" and it's not a bad trip at all. It has a good combination of ports (all of the major ones) as well as a considerable amount of scenic cruising. It doesn't provide anything out of the ordinary but it is a solid "first-timer's" Alaska trip. Most departures include Glacier Bay, and we suggest you try book-

The Right Cruise For You

ing one of those instead of the smaller number of departures that substitute Hubbard Glacier.

⚓ INFINITY

This brand-new ship offers a seven-night Inside Passage cruise departing from and returning to Vancouver.

ITINERARY: Cruising the Inside Passage, Juneau, Haines, Skagway, cruising Hubbard Glacier, and Ketchikan.

EVALUATION: Well, if you want to say that you sailed on one of the newest and most awesome ships now going to Alaska, you can take this cruise. Otherwise, it has little to offer. The port calls are standard for the Inside Passage run, although the stop at isolated Haines can be a plus for those who want to see a less touristy Alaskan port of call. Hubbard Glacier substitutes for Glacier Bay, not exactly what we consider the best way to go.

⚓ MERCURY

This ship offers a seven-night Gulf of Alaska cruise departing from Vancouver and ending in Seward, or the reverse itinerary.

ITINERARY: Cruising the Inside Passage, Ketchikan, Juneau, Skagway, cruising Hubbard Glacier and College Fjord, and a final port call at Valdez. The southbound itinerary does not sail through College Fjord and omits Valdez. Instead, it stops at Sitka.

EVALUATION: Considering that it's only a week long, this itinerary crams in quite a lot of nice sights. All of the major ports are there and the stop at Valdez on the northbound departures is something that many ships heading for Seward don't bother including. That's a plus. Another reason we prefer the northbound option is that it also sails through beautiful College Fjord. On the other hand, you have to settle on all sailings for Hubbard Glacier instead of Glacier Bay.

⚓ NORWEGIAN SKY

This ship offers an eight-day cruise through the Inside Passage from Seattle.

ITINERARY: Port calls are Victoria (British Columbia), Ketchikan, Juneau and Skagway. Scenic cruising consists of the Inside Passage and either Glacier Bay or the Sawyer Glacier.

EVALUATION: This itinerary is quite a bit different than most other round-trip Inside Passage cruises. Different, however, isn't necessarily better. The stop in Victoria is all right, although you'll only have about four hours during the evening, not the best way of seeing this delightful spot. You also don't do the full gamut of the Inside Passage, although that is virtually offset by the fact that the scenery upon leaving Seattle is just as good as in the Inside Passage. Sawyer Glacier isn't a common stop on most cruises – those that don't do Glacier Bay usually substitute Hubbard Glacier. Sawyer is beautiful but is no Glacier Bay nor is it even as spectacular as Hubbard. So, if you do select this cruise go for a departure that does Glacier Bay. The Seattle departure is interesting. It does avoid the bus trip to Vancouver since most of the cruise ships will not have you flying into Vancouver directly.

⚓ NORWEGIAN WIND

The *Norwegian Wind* has a round-trip from Vancouver on this largely typical eight-day Inside Passage cruise.

ITINERARY: The ports of call are Ketchikan, Juneau, Skagway and Haines. Scenic cruising of the Inside Passage and either Glacier Bay or Sawyer Glacier.

The Right Cruise For You

EVALUATION: As we just pointed out, this is a run-of-the-mill Inside Passage-only itinerary. The Haines stop makes it mildly interesting but Sitka would probably be better. If you get one of the departures that does Glacier Bay then it is as good as most other Inside Passage cruises. Sawyer Glacier is definitely not in the top 10 of Alaskan cruise attractions.

⚓ OCEAN PRINCESS

The Ocean Princess has a seven-day Gulf of Alaska cruise beginning in Vancouver and ending in Seward or the reverse.

ITINERARY and EVALUATION: See the listing under the *Dawn Princess*.

⚓ RADIANCE OF THE SEAS

This spanking new luxury liner offers an eight-day Inside Passage cruise departing from and returning to Vancouver.

ITINERARY: Cruising the Inside Passage, Juneau, Skagway, Haines, Hubbard Glacier, and Ketchikan.

EVALUATION: This is another standard Inside Passage itinerary that isn't great but isn't bad either. The only major port not visited is Sitka but many passengers will probably enjoy the small town atmosphere of Haines as much or even more. It doesn't do Glacier Bay or any other especially scenic cruising except for Hubbard Glacier.

⚓ REGAL PRINCESS

Offers an eight-day Inside Passage-only cruise beginning in Vancouver and returning to the same port.

ITINERARY: Cruising the Inside Passage and Hubbard Glacier. Port calls are Ketchikan, Juneau, Skagway and Sitka.

EVALUATION: No real complaints here considering that almost no Inside Passage cruise on the larger ships includes Glacier Bay these days. (You generally have to go on to the Gulf of Alaska for that.) This itinerary offers stops at the "big three" ports – Ketchikan, Juneau and Skagway – and adds in Sitka. A "no surprises" type cruise.

⚓ RHAPSODY OF THE SEAS

The Rhapsody handles the Gulf of Alaska cruises for Royal Caribbean this time around and offers an eight-day trip beginning in Vancouver and ending in Seward, or the reverse routing.

ITINERARY: Cruising the Inside Passage, Ketchikan, Skagway, Juneau, Sitka, and cruising Hubbard Glacier before arriving in Seward. The southbound itinerary also cruises Misty Fjords.

EVALUATION: Typical itinerary for this type of cruise and nothing special at all. Unfortunately, it omits both Glacier Bay and Valdez. Therefore, in order to maximize scenic cruising opportunities, we suggest going with the southbound option.

⚓ RYNDAM

Two eight-day cruises offered: Vancouver-Seward (or reverse) "Glacier Discovery" tour or a round-trip Inside Passage cruise.

ITINERARY: (1) "Glacier Discovery" – The northbound itinerary begins by cruising the Inside Passage, Ketchikan, Juneau, Sitka, Hubbard Glacier, Valdez and College Fjord. Southbound trips omit Hubbard Glacier and Valdez but, instead, cruise through Glacier Bay. (2) Cruises the Inside Passage and has port calls at Juneau, Skagway and Ketchikan besides scenic cruising through Glacier Bay.

EVALUATION: The "Glacier Discovery" route is a generally good itinerary that hits most of the important ports of call along with sailing through much of Alaska's best coastal scenery. The only omission of significance as far as ports are concerned is Skagway. We do have a slight preference for the southbound itinerary since it does Glacier Bay; however, the combination of Valdez and Hubbard Glacier in the other direction isn't that bad of an alternative. The *Ryndam's* Inside Passage itinerary is quite typical of the genre with the plus that it does visit Glacier Bay.

⚓ SEA PRINCESS

This Princess has the seven-day Gulf of Alaska run from Vancouver to Seward or the reverse itinerary.

ITINERARY and EVALUATION: See the listing under the *Dawn Princess* for details.

⚓ SEVEN SEAS MARINER

This ship has four different itineraries. The majority of the sailing dates are for eight days. There are a few 10- and 12-day trips, but if you want one of those you had best be careful to make sure it is given at a time you can arrange.

ITINERARY: The eight-day Inside Passage cruise from Vancouver to Vancouver sails the Inside Passage and Tracy Arm. It has port stops at Sitka, Juneau, Skagway and Ketchikan. The same length Gulf of Alaska itinerary begins in Seward. It cruises Hubbard Glacier, Tracy Arm and the Inside Passage, with the ports being Sitka, Juneau, Skagway and Ketchikan. Alternatively, the Gulf of Alaska options are a 10-day cruise that covers Victoria, the Inside Passage, Misty Fjords, Ketchikan, Juneau, Skagway, Sitka, Hubbard Glacier, Valdez and College Fjord. The 12-day version is the same, Alaska-wise, but also has a port call at Seattle.

EVALUATION: Either of the eight-day itineraries are basically solid trips that hit most of the high points. It's a little disappointing that this high-priced and relatively small ship doesn't include Glacier Bay, but at least you do get to see Misty Fjords. If you're going for one of the longer sailings, we think that the 10-day is a much better trip because the two extra days to get to and from Seattle (and to see that city) could be better spent as a pre- or post-cruise option.

⚓ STATENDAM

The *Statendam* has an eight-day Gulf of Alaska cruise that departs from Vancouver and ends in Seward, or the reverse direction.

ITINERARY: The northbound itinerary begins by cruising the Inside Passage, Ketchikan, Juneau, Sitka, Hubbard Glacier, Valdez and College Fjord. Southbound trips omit Hubbard Glacier and Valdez but, instead, cruise through Glacier Bay.

EVALUATION: This is a generally good itinerary that hits most of the important ports and does a lot of the best of coastal Alaska's scenic sights. The only significant omission as far as ports are concerned is Skagway. We have a slight preference for the southbound itinerary since it does Glacier Bay; however, the combination of Valdez and Hubbard Glacier in the other direction isn't that bad of an alternative.

⚓ SUN PRINCESS

Like the majority of the other Princess ships in Alaska for the summer of 2001, the *Sun Princess* features a seven-day Gulf of Alaska cruise from Vancouver to Seward or the reverse.

ITINERARY and EVALUATION: See the listing under the *Dawn Princess* for details.

The Right Cruise For You

⚓ VEENDAM

Offers a choice of two eight-day cruises: a Vancouver-Seward (or reverse) "Glacier Discovery" tour, or a round-trip Inside Passage cruise.

ITINERARY and EVALUATION: Since this ship offers the same choices of itineraries as the *Ryndam*, see the listing for that ship above for all the details.

⚓ VISION OF THE SEAS

Offers an eight-day Inside Passage cruise departing from and returning to Vancouver.

ITINERARY: Scenic cruising consists of Hubbard Glacier, Misty Fjords and the Inside Passage. Port calls are Ketchikan, Juneau, Haines and Skagway.

EVALUATION: We like this better than a lot of the other Inside Passage trips because it does do Misty Fjords, something not on the agenda for many of the larger ships. Royal Caribbean appears to have settled on Haines as a port call rather than Sitka for all its Inside Passage runs. While we would prefer Sitka, it isn't that big a deal. No doubt, a lot of Alaska visitors will prefer the far less commercialized atmosphere in Haines.

⚓ VOLENDAM, WESTERDAM & ZAANDAM

These three Holland America ships exclusively sail the eight-day Inside Passage route. They originate from and return to Vancouver.

ITINERARY: Ports of call are Juneau, Skagway and Ketchikan. Scenic sailing is highlighted by the Inside Passage and Glacier Bay.

EVALUATION: Fairly typical of most Inside Passage-only cruises, we have no big complaints about this nice itinerary. In an era where many of the big liners are not going to Glacier Bay it is nice that HAL still places importance on this bit of scenic cruising. That is, *all* departures include it. Since this isn't an overly long itinerary it could have been improved a bit by adding Sitka as a port call.

Small Ships

⚓ CLIPPER ODYSSEY

The 11-day "Intimate Perspective of Alaska" trip travels from Whittier (near Anchorage) to Prince Rupert, British Columbia. The 14-day "Crossroads of America & Asia" travels from Anchorage to Petropavlovsk, Russia. There is only one departure date for each itinerary.

ITINERARY: Intimate Perspective – Cruising Prince William Sound, Kayak Island, Gulf of Alaska, whale watching at Point Adolphus, Haines, Juneau, cruising the Tracy Arm and Inside Passage, Ketchikan, Prince of Wales Island, Misty Fjords National Monument. Crossroads – Anchorage, Nome, Gambell, St. Lawrence Island, Pribilof Island and several other far reaching islands, followed by a few stops in the Russian Far East.

EVALUATION: The Intimate Perspective trip is an excellent and detailed cruise for those whose priority is scenic cruising and wildlife over ports of call. Since that is definitely an appealing aspect of Alaska we can't find much fault with it. Just be certain that is the kind of Alaskan experience you are looking for. Certainly the Crossroads of America & Asia itinerary is one of the most unusual in the world of cruising. In the case of either itinerary, you are probably wise to have the cruise line make all of your air arrangements due to the limited flight schedules to and from some of the gateway locations.

⚓ EXECUTIVE EXPLORER

These eight-day cruises travel from Ketchikan to Juneau or reverse.

ITINERARY: After spending overnight in Ketchikan and allowing plenty of time to see the town, the ship cruises Misty Fjords and makes a stop at a small Native American village called Kake, then continues on to Sitka, Glacier Bay National Park, Haines, Skagway, cruising Tracy Arm. The reverse itinerary spends overnight in Juneau.

EVALUATION: An excellent Inside Passage itinerary since it doesn't have to do the least scenic portion of the passage between Vancouver (or wherever most cruises begin) and the Alaskan state line near Ketchikan. Kake is exclusive to Clipper Cruises and is interesting. Misty Fjords is always a plus. If you want to concentrate on Southeast Alaska and can do without the Gulf of Alaska then this itinerary is super. Do keep in mind, however, that air connections to and from Juneau or Ketchikan aren't as convenient as the more popular gateway cities.

⚓ SEA LION & SEA BIRD

Each of these ships has an eight-day "Coastal Alaska" itinerary beginning in Juneau and ending in Sitka (including transfer to Seattle by air). Like their larger counterparts, options including extensions to the interior of Alaska are available.

ITINERARY: Juneau is explored before embarkation. The cruise itinerary includes the Tracy Arm, Petersburg, Frederick Sound, Chatham Strait, Glacier Bay National Park, Chichagof Island. One day of cruising doesn't even have a specific itinerary. Activities will be geared towards what the passengers are most interested in and usually involve exploring some place well off the beaten path. Sitka is the last port call but is explored after disembarkation. You then fly to Seattle.

EVALUATION: The only major drawback (assuming you're happy with the small ship concept) is that the Gulf of Alaska is not on the itinerary. The exploration of Alaska's coastal waters is about as thorough as you can get even though Ketchikan and Skagway aren't ports of call. And that, for many travelers, is part of the attraction of this cruise. It doesn't concentrate on ports – the idea is to see coastal Alaska in its wildest and most natural form. It's an excellent trip, although probably more suited to the second-time Alaskan visitor rather than those seeking a more general visit to the Great Land. The emphasis is definitely on adventure travel of the soft variety, with lots of time spent in Zodiac rafts or shore walks.

⚓ UNIVERSE EXPLORER

This large "small ship" has two 15-day itineraries departing from and returning to Vancouver.

ITINERARY: The basic itinerary sails the Inside Passage and stops at Wrangell, Juneau, Skagway, Seward, Valdez, Sitka, Ketchikan and Victoria, British Columbia. It also sails the Gulf of Alaska, Glacier Bay and Hubbard Glacier. A few sailings vary the itinerary by not stopping at either Wrangell or Valdez, instead substituting Kodiak and Metlakatla.

EVALUATION: Either the basic or varied itinerary is one of the most comprehensive Alaska cruises available today and covers more ports and sights than any of the major cruise lines. The stop at Victoria is definitely a nice touch. The sailings that stop at Metlakatla and Kodiak are an interesting option. Both are rather out of the way places that few Alaska cruise tourists visit. Either is as interesting as Wrangell but we

The Right Cruise For You

feel Valdez is more worthwhile, so we would go with the basic itinerary. However, either way, it's a great itinerary and definitely worth considering.

⚓ WILDERNESS ADVENTURER

An eight-day cruise that begins and ends in Juneau. Connections to Juneau aren't as easy as to big cities but they're better than they are to Ketchikan or other Southeast Alaska towns.

ITINERARY: After departing Juneau on the second day, cruise Glacier Bay National Park, Point Adolphus and the Icy Strait, Chichagof and Baranof islands, Admiralty Island and the Tracy Arm.

EVALUATION: Like all the Glacier Bay Tours & Cruises, this one confines itself to the Inside Passage of Southeast Alaska. What is different about this trip is that, apart from Juneau, the itinerary does not include the usual ports of call. Rather, it concentrates on scenic cruising. If that's your entire cup of tea, then this is fine. However, we feel that for a first-time Alaska cruiser, a more general itinerary of scenic cruising and ports is a better way to get acquainted with Alaska. Experienced Alaskan cruisers might find this a more suitable experience.

⚓ WILDERNESS DISCOVERER

This eight-day cruise departs from Juneau and ends at Sitka, or the reverse itinerary.

ITINERARY: Overnight on board ship in Juneau and then cruising Tracy Arm, Skagway (including the Yukon and White Pass Railroad), Glacier Bay National Park, Icy Strait, and Baranof Island. A Sitka tour is included upon disembarkation. Reverse itineraries spend overnight on board in Sitka and have a post-cruise Juneau tour.

EVALUATION: In general, this cruise shares many similarities with that of the *Wilderness Adventurer*, but this one is better for the first-time Alaska traveler because there are three major ports (Juneau, Sitka and Skagway). The only major Inside Passage port that is omitted is Ketchikan, but this itinerary more than makes up for it with its unusual scenic cruising and inclusion of Glacier Bay National Park (as do *all* itineraries of this company's ships). Kayaking and shore walks on remote islands are part of this itinerary so those with a bit of adventure in their souls will do well to consider it.

⚓ WILDERNESS EXPLORER

This new routing offers a seven-day round-trip from the tiny port of Gustavus in Glacier Bay.

ITINERARY: Cruises the Icy Strait and Glacier Bay in depth. Kayaking and hiking are included activities.

EVALUATION: A soft-adventure type cruise good for the individual seeking to commune with nature in Alaska, who isn't interested in ports, history or much else besides. Except for a limited number of people who will absolutely love this type of trip (and you know who you are), the scenery on this trip can begin to get a little on the monotonous side, despite its beauty. It is worth noting that, for the intensive special interest cruises offered by Glacier Bay Cruises & Tours, there probably is no operator that does it better than they do. The thought also occurred to us that if you are traveling from point to point within Alaska via the Marine Highway System, this cruise could be a good way to break up that kind of journey. Flight connections into Gustavus aren't the most convenient.

The Right Cruise For You

⚓ YORKTOWN CLIPPER

The *Yorktown*'s 13-day trip embarks in Seattle and disembarks at Juneau. The 12-day excursion has the opposite routing as far as the starting and ending points, while the eight-day itinerary starts in Juneau and ends at Ketchikan.

ITINERARY: The 13-day trip cruises the Inside Passage, Misty Fjords National Monument, Ketchikan, Petersburg, Sawyer Glacier, cruising Tracy Arm, Sitka, Glacier Bay National Park, and various isolated islands. The 12-day trip is essentially the same trip in reverse. The eight-day excursion does Glacier Bay National Park, Sitka, cruising the Tracy Arm, Petersburg, Ketchikan, Misty Fjords National Monument and the Inside Passage.

EVALUATION: As is the general rule with the small ships, you get lots of detail in any such trip. The longer cruise is excellent in that it does a fine job of balancing the scenery and wildlife with stops in various ports large and small. We think it is well suited to the first-time Alaska visitor who has a little extra time. The shorter trip is definitely for the scenery lover, although it, too, has at least a smattering of port calls. You have to use a little imagination in scheduling flights to some of the embarkation/disembarkation locations, but for those looking for an in-depth Alaskan experience, that's a small price to pay.

Alaska Marine Highway Ferries

The AMH ferries don't have an "itinerary" in the usual sense of the word. They sail from one port to another and, depending on the route, may cover several ports. There are three basic route systems. The first is called the *Inside Passage,* or *South-*

east. Stops include cruise line ports like Skagway, Ketchikan, Juneau, Wrangell, Petersburg and Sitka, as well as a few really small communities that are otherwise reached only by some of the small ships. The Southeast system travels via Prince Rupert, British Columbia all the way to Bremerton, Washington. The latter is just a hop, skip and a jump from Seattle, so it is possible to trace virtually the entire Inside Passage routes followed by the cruise lines. The second route system goes under the name of *South Central* and serves Valdez, Cordova, Homer, Seward, Kodiak and Whittier, among others, all along the Gulf of Alaska and the Kenai Peninsula. It also connects into Anchorage. Unfortunately, the two systems are not connected, which means that if you want to do both you have to fly from the end of one to the beginning of the other. The final system is the *Southwest*. This connects with the South Central at Kodiak and goes to various ports in the Aleutian Island chain. Since that is not on the usual Alaska visitor path we won't delve any further into it. However, as long as you know it's there, the possibility of touring the isolated island chain is open to you. For your information, the Bremerton, Washington terminal is located off of I-5, Exit 250.

TERMINAL LOCATIONS	
Inside Passage/Southeast Routes	
Ketchikan	2.5 miles north of downtown on main road.
Juneau	14 miles north of downtown on main road.
Petersburg	0.9 miles south of downtown on main road.
Sitka	7.1 miles north of downtown on main road.
Skagway	3 blocks south of downtown on main road.
Wrangell	2 blocks north of downtown on main road.

TERMINAL LOCATIONS	
South Central (Gulf of Alaska Routes)	
Anchorage	605 West 4th Avenue
Cordova	4 blocks north of downtown on main road.
Homer	4558 Homer Spit Road
Kodiak	100 Marine Way
Seward	At the Alaska Railroad dock.
Valdez	West end of the city dock.

The ferries provide the ultimate in flexibility if you have plenty of time. But, because they don't run often you could well find yourself finishing everything there is to see and do in Town A and then have to wait a whole day for the next ferry to come along to head on to Town B. If this doesn't seem like a problem to you, then you are among those who can seriously consider the ferry alternative.

One potential pitfall of traveling by ferry is the limited hotel facilities in many of the smallest towns. Again, unless you have almost unlimited time, it requires very careful planning to work out a schedule. The plus side is that you can visit every port, significant or otherwise, using this method.

Travelers who intend to use the AMH system should take note that the ferry dock is almost never located in the same place where cruise ships either tie up or send their tenders to. Most terminals are a short walk from the center of town. For those that aren't, you can easily get into town via taxi. Some of the larger communities also have bus service. In addition, since ferry passengers might well be staying in town, check with your hotel; many will provide transportation to the ferry dock.

Make Sure It's What You Want

Any Alaska sailing, whether it's by super-liner, intimate small vessel or even the mundane ferry, will leave you in awe at the products of Mother Nature. Our attempt here was to inform you about the many options available. In conjunction with your personal interests and preferences for the type of ship you travel on and the style of travel that is most suited to you and your budget, you should be able to make a choice that will satisfy the most important of all travel critics – you!

Activities During Alaska Cruising

We've already touched on some of the activities that occur on board cruise ships going to Alaska. For the most part, cruise ships in Alaska offer the same activities as cruises anywhere in the world. Most of you already know the standard offerings, so we'll concentrate on two areas: those activities unique to an Alaska cruise and, secondly, those found on almost all cruises, but often ignored or only briefly mentioned in most travel guides.

For some people, the option to relax and do nothing is attractive. Alternatively, you can swim, exercise, walk or jog around the deck, dance the night away, watch a movie, wine and dine until you explode, or be entertained by singers, dancers, comedians, magicians and who knows what else.

Each ship's daily calendar will inform you of scheduled dance lessons, card games or a dozen other activities, one or more of which is sure to whet your appetite.

The Right Cruise For You

Don't forget that it won't get dark until late, so there's plenty of time for seeing the sights as well.

Most cruise lines arrange to have experts on various aspects of Alaskan geography and culture on board, most often Alaskan residents. They provide lectures, video or slide presentations, and discussion groups that should be informative to anyone interested in learning about Alaska. They're also available as reference sources should you have a question. Many times their lectures take the form of a briefing on sights and items of interest in an upcoming port of call. The nature and frequency of these events will vary from ship to ship. You should find the time to attend as many of these meetings as possible – it will almost always be time well spent.

Every ship will have a tour office to answer questions and help arrange sightseeing excursions ashore. Most ships hold a briefing on excursions very early in the cruise and, even if you know what you want to do in each port, these talks are still informative. Make your decisions on optional tours as early as possible since they tend to fill up quickly. Ideally, you should have everything booked by the morning following your embarkation. Several cruise lines will provide you with information on shore tours prior to sailing and will allow you to reserve all or some of them before departure. Best in this category is Princess, which not only gives you full information about more than 80 optional tour itineraries, but allows you to book them before you sail. Your tour tickets will be waiting for you when you arrive at your stateroom, eliminating the need to stand in line at the ship's tour office. As of press time, Princess was the only line to offer this convenient service, but we're sure that its instant popularity with Princess passengers will not go unnoticed by the other major cruise lines.

Another important group of activities involves touring the ship itself. Most cruise ships offer passengers an opportunity to look behind the scenes and see how the ship is operated. While the availability and scope of these tours varies, most will show you around the huge and spotless kitchens where your extravagant meals are prepared.

Open house on the bridge is also a well-attended event, where children and adults can make believe they are the captain for at least a few moments. Notification of these activities is generally given to passengers well in advance. If they haven't been announced, inquire of your ship's steward; you'll probably find these tours are available.

Before leaving the topic of activities on larger ships, we should take a moment to address an increasingly popular aspect of cruising in general that also applies to Alaska journeys – the theme cruise. This is simply a cruise where many of the passenger activities are built around a particular theme. The variety of topics is amazingly varied and can cover the gamut from anthropology to zoology and everything in-between. Other examples might include music appreciation, investments and finance, or sports and fitness. Obviously, most themes don't have any affect on the ship's itinerary because the theme is most often totally unrelated to the destination. A theme cruise doesn't necessarily make an Alaskan cruise any better for the average traveler. However, if you find a theme that interests you, then it can help to make for more pleasant shipboard activities for those times when you're not in port and on-deck sightseeing is in a lull.

The smaller the ship, of course, the fewer activities and facilities. Don't expect all manner of activities on small explorer-type ships. With few exceptions, they have only onboard Alaska experts. In fact, the availability of knowledgeable local experts is a hallmark of the small ship experience.

The Right Cruise For You

Options in Port:
Package Tours vs. On Your Own

What you must decide is when a guided tour is better than heading out on your own. Information to help you come to the best decision is described in the chapter entitled *Ports of Call & Cruise Sightseeing*. For now, however, there are several observations to keep in mind.

▶ All ports, including the capital city of Juneau, are relatively small. In-town sightseeing can be done on your own and on foot. We don't recommend spending money on a guided bus tour, unless you need to because of physical limitations.

▶ Several stops, notably Juneau, Sitka, Ketchikan and Skagway, do have roads that extend a few miles from town (and much farther in the case of Skagway) and provide access to many other wonderful sights. In these instances it's often less expensive to rent a car for the day (the part of the day you'll be in port) than to take a guided tour. All of the towns mentioned have car rentals available; advance reservations would be wise.

▶ There are situations where the package tours visit places that you can't get to on your own, either because the public at large isn't admitted, or the transportation method requires being with a group or guide. Most common in this group are such diverse activities as river rafting (both scenic and whitewater), helicopter or float plane tours, and fishing expeditions.

This brings us to the matter of air tours. There's something intangible about this type of sightseeing adventure – it's certainly more exciting than riding around in a bus! Helicopters and float planes are the main conveyances employed. You'll get a unique view of the dramatic scenery and, more importantly, you'll be visiting the places that aren't otherwise accessible. A trip lasting an hour will almost certainly set you back well over $200 per person. Whether that is worth it to you is a personal call. The biggest potential pitfall with these excursions is the weather. If conditions won't permit a safe trip, the excursion will be canceled and your money will be cheerfully refunded. Well, refunded for sure. At other times it may be safe to go, but the weather may not be ideal for viewing. It is frustrating to encounter poor visibility on these trips, but it is not an uncommon occurrence.

Some Alternative Modes of Getting Around

As this book is about *cruising* Alaska, we won't get heavily involved in overland adventures except for what is common either prior to or after a cruise. However, a few interesting other journeys that involve both may be of interest to many readers.

TAUCK TOURS

This is one of the most respected names in the group-escorted travel business. They offer eight- and 13-day air/land/sea trips through the Inside Passage via Holland America Line or on the *Yorktown Clipper* and into the interior by train or motor coach, depending upon the itinerary. Prices begin at about $2,600 for the shorter journey and $5,000 for the longer. By the way, Tauck can get you a significant discount on any Holland America Line cruise if you take any Tauck Tour.

MAUPINTOURS

The fierce business rival of Tauck, Maupintour has an interesting Alaskan/Yukon itinerary that lasts 12 days and costs about $3,225 per person. Included are Anchorage, the Alaska Railroad, Denali and Fairbanks. It then travels the Alaska and Klondike Highways to visit Dawson City and Skagway via the White Pass & Yukon Railroad. It isn't a cruise vacation, however, since the only time spent on the water is a cruise through Glacier Bay and a ferry trip to the tour's ending point in Juneau.

ALASKA HIGHWAY CRUISES

Offers an interesting combination trip. You take either an Inside Passage or Inside Passage/Gulf of Alaska cruise on Holland America Line and explore the interior via motor home. Trips range from nine to 22 days, with prices beginning at around $2,000 and going over $5,000. The itineraries (including the motor home portion) are pre-arranged, but there are so many options that it effectively is an individual tour (except for the cruise portion). Alaska Highway Cruises also offers many optional trips and tours that are essentially like the shore excursions available on the cruise tours. Finally, AHC's parent company operates a fishing lodge in the wilds, heaven for the enthusiastic angler.

ALASKA SIGHTSEEING/CRUISE WEST

This company's trips – both along the Inside Passage and Gulf of Alaska – may be more suited to the individual who is apprehensive about spending a lot of time on board ship. Cruise West features several one-day and/or overnight sailing from a number of locations that cover just about the full range of destinations available on longer cruises. They even have several tours into the interior, including Denali National Park.

Practical
Information

Alaska is different. Although you may have done your research and decided where to go, the season in which to travel and even what to pack, there may be some things you are still unsure of.

Weather/Clothing On & Off Ship

Don't let the beautiful full-color pictures in the cruise brochures fool you. Sunny days are the exception rather than the rule, although prolonged hard rains are relatively rare in the summer. You may enjoy the cool temperatures on deck, but be aware that chilling winds can pick up as the ship starts moving. Pack some warm jackets if you intend to whale-watch all day! Don't let this deter you one bit: rained-out activities are few and far between and, if you're suitably dressed, you can laugh at the weather. Alaskans, mindful of copious amounts of water from the sky, refer to rain as liquid sunshine. And there is a bonus to the cloudy weather – the beauty of the glaciers is enhanced by it. Their ice-blue color is intense under cloud cover, much more so than if the sun is shining brightly.

Then they appear white. You must also consider the unpredictable nature of Alaskan weather. Seeing clouds now does not mean it won't be much nicer in a short time. (A very common Alaskan reaction to visitors who complain about the weather is that if you don't like the current conditions just wait five minutes!)

CLIMATE CHART	MAY	JULY	SEPTEMBER
	High/Low/Rain	High/Low/Rain	High/Low/Rain
Ketchikan	56°/40°/4.2"	66°/48°/5.0"	57°/43°/6.9"
Juneau	55°/38°/3.4"	64°/47°/4.1"	56°/42°/6.4"
Skagway	59°/37°/2.0"	67°/49°/1.5"	60°/43°/3.7"
Anchorage	54°/38°/0.5"	65°/49°/1.5"	56°/40°/2.7"
Fairbanks	58°/37°/0.7"	71°/50°/1.9"	56°/35°/1.2"

The best advice on clothing is to pack for just about anything. Dress in layers so that you can quickly adapt to changing conditions. You should wear clothes of a casual nature, including some warm woolens, a heavy sweater, hat and gloves. A fairly heavy outer jacket is also advisable. A lightweight waterproof jacket comes in handy for intermittent showers.

These suggestions apply to time in port as well as on board ship. The reality in Alaska is that on a moving ship (or one that is standing still near the foot of a glacier) temperatures will be cool.

All the ships will provide blankets to wrap yourself in, but these can be hard to manage while you're taking pictures or videos.

Always bundle up warm. That way, you have the option to peel off layers as the climate determines.

Dining

Fine dining, and lots of it, is one of the true delights of cruising for many people. In the ship listings provided earlier we offered a quick summation of each ship's dining regimen. Now is the time to look a little more closely at what this means. Traditionally, most ships offered a formal dinner in the main dining room with passengers choosing whether they preferred early or late seating. The same was true for breakfast and lunch, although these meals were often open seating – that is you came as you pleased within a previously announced time frame. However, since many passengers want to get a quick start in the morning or are in port during lunch, the majority of large ships also had buffet options for both breakfast and lunch. This is still the case on every ship. Unfortunately, the more relaxed single-seating for dinner seems to be largely a thing of the past except on the most exclusive ships. But, on the bright side, more and more ships are now offering an expanded range of dining options for dinner. Almost all of the larger ships have at least one other specialty restaurant (and frequently several) to choose from. This means that you can have dinner in the main dining room one night, go Italian the next, and opt for a quaint little bistro-style café on another. All of the other restaurants are usually on a walk-in or reservation basis so you aren't restricted to a particular seating time.

Dinner attire on each cruise ship falls into three categories: (1) casual; (2) dressy, now usually called "informal"; and (3) formal. The non-cruise liners (i.e., smaller explorer boats) are almost always casual every night.

▶ *Casual* means no tie or jacket for men, and women can wear slacks or a simple dress. The most formal

Practical Information

of ships have at least a couple of casual nights during the course of a cruise, while others are casual more often than not. Remember that neither shorts nor sandals are acceptable at dinner.

▶ *Informal* requires that men wear a jacket (tie requirements vary) and women should wear dresses or pant suits. The majority of cruise liners observe this mode for dinner on most nights.

▶ The *formal* category theoretically means a tuxedo for men and gowns for women. However, that's only a recommendation from the cruise lines, who seem to think that everyone enjoys getting all dressed up for dinner, even in the wilderness of Alaska. Men will be admitted for dinner (even for the very formal Captain's dinner) if they wear a dark suit. Be advised that the majority of men will be wearing tuxedos, however, so you might feel uncomfortable being in the underdressed suit minority. Many larger ships provide tuxedo rentals. In reality, no one will say anything or care how you dress. The same goes for the ladies. A nice dress (but not slacks) will be acceptable in lieu of a gown.

Dress for events in the later evening hours is the same as for dinner since very few people, if any, will bother changing their clothes after dinner.

The Cruising Season

With the limitations imposed by Alaska's weather, the cruising season is quite short, generally running from mid-May to mid-September. Prices are highest in July and August and lowest at the beginning and end of each season. Most cruises have a mid-price range for a short time (usually one or two departures) between the high and low periods. Consult individual cruise line brochures or your travel agent for exact dates and rates.

Before deciding that you want to save money by traveling on the fringes of the cruise season, remember that it can really be cold at these times, with temperatures frequently falling below freezing and precipitation sometimes being in the form of snow. It's necessary to weigh the cost savings against the greater possibility of being uncomfortable. July and August definitely offer the best weather.

Discounts, Flight Arrangements & Cruise Tours

Almost every cruise ship line offers a price reduction for booking early. Some offer a cash discount, which may begin at around $200 for lower-priced staterooms and rise to approximately $1,000 for the more expensive accommodations. This usually applies to bookings made in January and February. A new trend is to discount March and even April bookings, but only by about half as much as for the earlier period. Other lines give a percentage off the regular fare. This amount varies by line, but can be as much as 25%. A smaller discount of around 10% is offered by some for reservations made prior to the end of April.

Bargains are sometimes available at the last minute if rooms are empty. However, it's taking a big chance to wait until then and advance reservations are highly recommended.

Practical Information

81

You may be able to save money by contacting a discount agent who buys up large blocks of staterooms. Newspaper travel sections often have advertisements of this nature. Make sure, however, that the outfit you're dealing with is reliable – they should be a member of CLIA (Cruise Lines International Association). If you have any doubts about a discounter, contact **CLIA** at 500 Fifth Avenue, suite, 1407, New York, NY 10110. One recommended discount broker that we know is reliable is **Cruises of Distinction, ☎** (800) 634-3445.

Package deals that include air fares from almost anywhere in the United States and Canada are another money-saving possibility. For example, an additional $600 or so to the cost of your cruise will provide round-trip air transportation from New York to Vancouver and a return flight to New York from Anchorage. In some cases if you opt not to use the cruise line's air program you will receive a credit on the cruise package fare. Very often, flights from West Coast gateway cities are completely free of charge. In all cases, when you use the add-on or free air programs you must travel on flights that have been designated by the cruise line, although most lines will now arrange for specific flights that you request. However, there is an additional charge for this service. The cruise lines use scheduled flights on major carriers but they may not be at the most convenient time for you. Additionally, the flights often are not the most direct routings.

The majority of cruise passengers do utilize the cruise line air programs but this is not always the best way to go. Although the brochures will lead you to believe that you're getting a real bargain on the cost of air, that is all too often far from the truth. Find out what the cost will be for air from the cruise line and then see what you can get on your own. Don't be surprised if you find that much lower costs are available elsewhere. If you make your own air arrangements you will have to provide your own transfers from the airport to the cruise ship and reverse. Do factor that into the total cost. And remember to keep in mind that even if your own arrangements come out a few dollars higher, it may be well worth it because you get to pick the airline and flight schedule that is best for you.

Since many Alaskan cruise passengers will be going to Alaska only once in their lives, it isn't surprising that a high percentage of cruisers also choose to combine their cruise with other Alaska destinations or sightseeing in the Pacific Northwest. All lines offer numerous packages either before or after the cruise. Suggested itineraries for other parts of Alaska and the Pacific Northwest will be found in the chapter *Beyond the Cruise*. You might want to consider some of these packages if you like escorted group travel. However, if you prefer to be independent, you can do so easily with a little planning.

The largest cruise lines in Alaska, most notably Princess and Holland America, have the most extensive land program (and, therefore, will be the most likely to try to "push" them on you at the time you book your cruise). In the last couple of years even the lines that don't have the extensive Alaska schedule of those two companies have been increasing their options considerably. These can be group or individual travel or a combination of both. Most involve a trip on the Alaska Railroad to Denali National Park and Fairbanks. Both cruise lines book up whole cars on the train and you get first-class accommodations in special dome cars with the cruise line's name on it. Each has a land-based touring company and owns accommodations throughout Alaska (Princess Lodges and HAL's Westmark hotels). The two giants have been doing battle over the past few years, with Princess claiming that Holland America concentrates their land tours too much on the Yukon and not enough on Alaska. Holland America's Westours division counters that Yukon history is inseparable from that of Alaska. As historians, we have to agree with them on that score. But the whole fight is rather absurd – each line offers plenty of options in both Alaska and the Yukon.

The biggest decision you have to make regarding destinations you wish to see prior to or after the cruise is whether or not to book it as a cruise-tour through the cruise line, or to book the cruise separately and do everything else on your own. There is something to be said for both methods. The chief advantage of doing it on your own is having the flexibility to do exactly what you want and when you want to do it. On the other hand, cruise-tours offer experienced guides and continue the camaraderie that often develops during a cruise. Those considerations aside, the other important factor is price. If you read through all of the cruise line brochures they make it seem like these package tours are practically being given away! Well, nothing could be further from the truth. Our experience is that you could almost certainly do better cost-wise on your own.

So, we suggest the following method of selection. First, go through the cruise-tours and find the itinerary that is most to your liking. If it covers everything or almost everything you would opt to see on your own proceed to the next step – pricing it out. Figure out what it would cost on your own (transportation, lodging, meals, admissions, etc.) and compare that to what the cruise line is asking. If it's close, then go with the cruise-tour unless you are averse to group travel. But we think that the chances are good that you could save a substantial amount on your own. That is the way to do it unless you have a low confidence level when it comes to independent travel. However, if that were the case you probably wouldn't even bother to make the price comparison in the first place.

A final thought regarding your Alaska adventure. We've always been inclined to make our own reservations for most types of travel. You can certainly do the same for your cruise as every line has a customer service number for reservations. However, a cruise to Alaska is an expensive proposition and you will likely have lots of questions even after reading a book like this, especially if it's your first cruise. Therefore, the services of a good travel agent can be a real plus. Any reputable travel agent will do, but we strongly urge that you consider using the services of an agent who specializes in cruises. There are many of these throughout the country. One of the largest and best known is **Cruise Holidays**. Call ☎ (800) 866-7245 or visit their website at www.cruiseholidays.com to find a Cruise Holidays office near you.

Customs

Although a few cruises start from the United States, the majority begin in Vancouver, British Columbia. You'll have to go through Canadian Customs upon your arrival in Vancouver (or other point of entry). Then you must clear US Customs upon arrival in your first port of call back in the United States, which in most cases is Ketchikan. The southbound cruises encounter customs in the reverse sequence, but you'll still have to cross the same borders. More often than not this border crossing doesn't involve anything more than saying good morning to the Customs Inspector (you won't even see him or her when clearing Customs on the ship), but do be prepared to declare what you have purchased and, of course, have proof of your citizenship. A passport, although not required for American or Canadian citizens on an Alaska cruise, is always the best form of identification. A birth certificate with a picture ID, such as a valid driver's license, will also do.

Things to Take Along

In addition to the clothing suggestions discussed earlier on page 78, there are a few other items you should plan on bringing along. These include:

> ▶ A good pair of **binoculars** is perhaps the most important item. They allow you close-ups of spectacular glaciers and wildlife. Sometimes it's just as

Practical Information

easy to spot wildlife without binoculars, but the binoculars will bring it breathtakingly close.

▶ A **camera** is another absolute must. These days camcorders are just as commonplace. In either case, make sure you bring loads of film and blank tapes because you'll be snapping or filming at every turn. Extra battery packs are a good idea as the colder weather can sometimes reduce the life of your battery. While all accessories are available during your cruise, prices are certain to be lower where you live. You don't have to worry about film being damaged by heat in Alaska, so bring it all along with you. A good general-purpose film speed makes the most sense, since you will often be taking pictures under overcast skies.

▶ Alaskan summers are known for, among other things, a very large volume of insects whose voracious appetite can be quite annoying. Although insects are far less prominent in the southern panhandle and anywhere along the coast, you might encounter them in port. If you're going to be traveling to Denali, Fairbanks or anywhere else in the interior, then **insect repellent** is strongly recommended. Preparations that don't contain DEET are safer, especially for children.

▶ While cloudy weather is common, you can also expect to see sunshine at least some of the time. Therefore, **sunglasses** will also come in handy.

▶ Life aboard ship is cashless, except for tips (and often they, too, can be charged to your room account). You should bring along enough cash to cover gratuities and a small amount for expenditures in port. **Credit cards** are as common in Alaska as anywhere else. You'll be given guidance as to amounts that are considered appropriate to give to your dining room staff, stateroom attendant, and so on. Keep in mind that the service level is equal to or better than the finest hotels and restaurants. And, like the staff in those places, the crew depends upon tips for a large part of their income.

▶ Finally, always be sure to bring along a sufficient supply of any **medications** that you may be on in their original containers. A copy of the prescription is also handy should you lose your medicine (and for the occasional cranky Customs Officer). Common medicines are available on the ship, but most will have to be replaced in port. If you wear prescription eyeglasses, bring a spare set.

Traveling with Children

What used to be mainly an adult leisure activity (especially in Alaska) has now become something for the entire family, and many cruise lines actively cater to little ones. While small children may not be particularly interested in the sights and activities of Alaska, and there isn't any Disney line here, onboard programs for children are extensive on every cruise line. There shouldn't be any trouble keeping them occupied under supervision day or night. The individual cruise lines can answer any specific concerns you may have about traveling with children. Small ships are far less suitable for children under 17 than the multi-activity mega-liners.

So, It's Your First Time Cruising...

No need for concern, although we're sure that raises some additional questions in your mind. Being on a cruise ship is really

Practical Information

like staying at a moving full-service resort property. Most things are done for you, including bringing your luggage to and from your room upon embarkation and disembarkation. Every cruise line will provide you with lots of written material about the ship, its schedule and activities. Review what they give you. If you can't find the answer to a question, feel free to ask a crew member. They're always eager to please. Here a few items that you should be aware of:

▶ **Seasickness** is extremely unlikely on Alaska cruises because you aren't out on the high seas and summer storms are infrequent. However, if you're especially prone to motion sickness, an ounce of prevention can be useful. Remedies are available over the counter or by prescription, but they're effective only if you take them several hours prior to commencing your journey. If you haven't taken any preventive medication but are starting to feel the ill effects of motion sickness coming on, there are still some things you can do. If your symptoms are severe enough to prevent you from going about your activities, then it is best to lie down in a dark room with a cool cloth over your eyes or forehead. Another "home remedy" that helps some people is to hold an ice cube behind your ear. Minor symptoms can be somewhat alleviated by relaxing and gazing at a distant object, such as the horizon. Never look at something close, like the water over the railing of the side of the ship.

▶ While delays along the route can occur at any time, cruise lines are generally known for their punctuality. At each port of call they will give you a **time schedule** as to when you are to be back on board. Do comply! Although they may take attendance to see if everyone is back on the ship they will leave without you if you're still out wandering around in town somewhere or are exploring the wilderness.

▶ **Safety** is of utmost importance to the ship's crew. Pertinent instructions are posted in each stateroom. Every cruise will have a lifeboat drill on the first full day out. You are required to attend. It's unlikely that you'll ever have to use this information, but don't use that as a reason to skip class. You should be fully aware of emergency procedures, as should your children. And besides, the drill (you don't actually get into the lifeboats) is kind of fun and colorful with everyone wearing their orange life vests.

▶ **Tipping** of your dining room staff, stateroom attendant and other members of the crew is often a big question for first-time cruisers. Except for the rare "no tipping" policy sometimes found on the most expensive ships, the folding favor is a way of life on board ship. Every cruise line will include in your documentation package some suggestions on how much to tip each of the people who will be serving you during your cruise. These are *suggestions* and you should feel free to raise or lower the amounts depending upon your budget and how you feel about the service you received. However, they do offer a good starting point on which to base your decision. Tips to people who serve you throughout the trip (such as waiters and cabin attendants) are not given on a daily basis but at the end of the cruise. While these individuals do depend on tips for their livelihood, remember that you should *never* offer a gratuity to an officer of the ship.

Practical Information

Accommodations On Land

Almost every traveler to Alaska will probably spend at least a couple of nights in a hotel either before or after the cruise. We've included a few suggested places to stay in the most commonly visited tour add-on cities, such as Anchorage and Fairbanks, as well as Denali National Park. For the benefit of ferry travelers and others who aren't on the major cruise ships, we've added Homer, Seward and Valdez in the Gulf of Alaska, and all Inside Passage ports. You may also want to contact some of the major chain hotels to find out about additional lodging establishments. A list of such companies with a significant presence in Alaska is included in the *Addenda*.

Alaska is among the most expensive places to stay. Since prices seem to change with alarming regularity, we've established a range system rather than giving exact rates. Prices are based on double occupancy per night,and include state and local taxes.

Hotel Rates	
$$$$	Over $200
$$$	$160-199
$$	$100-159
$	Less than $100

Time of Day

All of Alaska (except for a small part of the Aleutian Island chain in the extreme southwestern portion of the state not visited by cruise ships) is on Alaska Standard Time. This is one hour *earlier* than the West Coast of the lower 48 states.

Cruise Lines & The Environment

The late 1990s were not a particularly good time for the cruise lines when it came to being environmentally friendly. Several major companies (we won't point fingers here because the guilt was pretty well spread around) received public relations black-eyes when it became publicly known that the cruise ships were illegally dumping waste into pristine Alaskan waters... waters that they always featured in their advertising. The cruise lines constantly spoke in green terms but their actions belied the image they were trying so hard to promote.

The bad publicity had more effect on correcting the problem than the efforts of any government or environmental group, individually or collectively. Regulation of ships is largely through international organizations and oversight is often slippery. The cruise lines have, for the most part, successfully resisted imposition of higher standards. However, in "voluntary" association, all of the lines have now undertaken serious efforts to reduce dumping, legal or otherwise. The newer ships are being designed to be more fuel efficient and have better on-board waste treatment facilities, so what is dumped into the water isn't as wretched as it used to be. So, if you are an environmentally conscious individual you can be somewhat optimistic that the worst is over. And now, the larger ships don't necessarily mean more pollution. With their more advanced technological systems they will often pollute far less than a smaller but older ship.

Further Information

Throughout this chapter we've mentioned names of cruise lines, airlines, tour operators and much more. You'll find a complete reference list of these and other good sources of in-

Practical Information

formation in the *Addenda*. Addresses and telephone numbers are included along with websites.

Ports of Call & Cruise Sightseeing

Not all ports are visited by every ship, but for the sake of simplicity we'll describe all ports and points of scenic interest that can be reached by cruise ship, large and small, as if you were traveling north from Vancouver to Anchorage.

You'll be given daily calendars onboard that will tell you about the port schedule as well as sightseeing and activities. It's best to be ready to disembark as soon as possible after docking to maximize the time available for sightseeing. (This is especially important if your ship uses tenders in most ports – lines of passengers waiting to get into town can sometimes develop.) When the time arrives for shipboard touring, do be ready as well. Your card game or gym workout should wait for a time when nothing spectacular is happening outside. Don't be surprised, however, when at dinner the conversation is about some magnificent scenery and your neighbor says, "I didn't see it because I was at the beauty salon." It happens on every cruise!

Time in port varies, but it's generally sufficient to see what's worthwhile. There will be occasions where lunch or dinner falls in the middle of your stay in port. When this happens there is almost always enough time to return and eat, then continue sightseeing. Don't forget that in summer darkness doesn't arrive until 11 pm in Alaska, so daytime activities such as sightseeing can be enjoyed well into the evening.

Note: Shore excursions and tours offered to passengers don't vary much at all from one cruise line to another as they are often operated by local companies and not the cruise lines.

The Inside Passage/Misty Fjords/Tracy Arm

The Inside Passage is visualized by the inexperienced traveler as the waterway alongside the southern Alaskan panhandle. Actually, it is much more than that. It extends for approximately 950 miles from Seattle, Washington to Skagway, Alaska and serves as a busy year-round shipping lane. The passage is protected by a series of islands large and small. These islands afford two advantages for the traveler. First, rough seas associated with ocean travel are an extreme rarity here. Second, you never lose sight of land, which means there is always something to see. This is unlike an ocean voyage where the blue sea, although undeniably beautiful in its own right, can sometimes become rather tedious after a few days at sea.

Almost all Alaska-bound liners leave from the cruise ship terminal in downtown Vancouver, usually around six in the evening. From aboard your ship, take time to admire the structure of the terminal building, whose design resembles that of a sailing ship. As you sail through the busy harbor on the Burrard

Inlet you'll also have a great view of Vancouver's beautiful skyline. You say good-bye to the city shortly after sailing beneath the First Narrows Bridge, also known as the Lion's Bridge. From there it's into the Strait of Georgia as you begin your passage north.

Your first full day aboard ship will be spent traversing the Canadian portion of the Inside Passage along the mountainous shoreline of the province of British Columbia. You get a better view of the mountains later, but for now, enjoy the pleasant scenery – a rocky shoreline covered with lush green vegetation due to the Pacific Northwest's rainy climate. Sometimes you'll be able to spot some small towns along the coast, but settlements are quite scattered and become more so as the voyage continues. It's natural that many passengers are anxious to spend some time on deck the first day, but because of the limited sights in this part of the journey you'll probably wind up devoting more time acquainting yourselves with the facilities and layout of the ship. There's a lot to explore onboard, and now is a good time to do so as the scenery will only get better the farther north you go. But, among the sights you should be on the lookout for on the first day out are the many picturesque islands in the narrow inlets near the town of Bella Bella on the British Columbia coast and in attractive Alert Bay.

By the following day the scenery becomes outstanding. Once you near Misty Fjords the coastal mountain peaks that form the border between the United States and Canada are generally around 6,500 feet high. These continue to rise and, by the time you approach Juneau, many exceed 7,500 feet. The Devil's Paw, located east of Juneau, is an immense 8,554 feet high. If you're thinking that you've seen higher mountains, just remember that since you are viewing them from sea level their height is even more impressive. (For example, a 14,000-foot peak in the Rockies viewed from Colorado Springs is about 8,000 feet higher than your vantage point – about equal to some of the increases in altitude that you will view along the Inside Passage!)

The narrow strip of land that forms the Alaskan panhandle mainland averages only about 30 miles in width (beyond which is Canadian territory) from north of Misty Fjords until it ends at Skagway. The forested mountains and the waters of the Inside Passage aren't the only sights. Ice-capped peaks are everywhere and you'll probably also spot your first glaciers and ice floes, although they'll be quite small. The waterfalls, too numerous to count, will frequently cascade down the rocky slopes on both shores and are striking sights. Many have the appearance of thin silver threads, while others are torrents that gush into the cold greenish waters of the Inside Passage.

Misty Fjords

Located just over the Canadian border, the Misty Fjords National Monument covers a vast tract of land bordered for more than 60 miles by the Behm Canal (a natural waterway – the word canal in its name and in many other channels of the Inside Passage is a misnomer), which is only three miles wide. The narrowness of the passage enhances the many sea cliffs and sheer walls, which in some places rise more than 3,000 feet. Mountains enclose the canal on every side. The sound and sight of rushing waterfalls is everywhere. Its name is appropriate to the most common weather condition here. While this can severely hamper a flightseeing visit, it presents only a minor setback for cruise ships. In fact, the mist that envelops the fjords adds to the atmosphere and beauty of the natural surroundings.

The Tracy Arm

This inlet, one of dozens scattered along the entire length of the Inside Passage, is 40 miles south of Juneau. It has been singled out from many others as a detour for cruise ships because of its special charm. It's more than 20 miles long and only a couple miles wide. The fjord, entered via Holkham Bay, is surrounded by high mountains and the abundance of waterfalls here is even greater than in most areas of the Inside Passage that you've been traveling on so far. If you haven't already caught a glimpse of an iceberg, you will probably see one here as it floats peacefully in the waters of Tracy Arm. For those of you whose ship might be visiting Endicott Arm instead of Tracy, it branches off the same bay as the Tracy Arm and provides very similar scenery. In either case, as the first fjord that most ships come to, it will be something that always remains fresh in your mind.

Ketchikan

The local chamber of commerce proudly proclaims that "Alaska begins in Ketchikan," and it's geographically correct to say so. After you cross the Canadian border, Ketchikan will be the first stop. The town has also designated itself the "Salmon Capital of the World," based not only on its origins as a cannery town back in 1887, but because that industry is still of great importance to the local economy. With a population of about 14,000 people, Ketchikan is the fourth-largest city in Alaska, which tells you something about the size of the 49th state's cities!

The Ketchikan area runs for 31 miles along Tongass Narrows, with downtown stretching for three miles. Like many other towns along the Inside Passage, Ketchikan is long and very narrow – often only a few blocks wide. This is because the coastal mountains along the Alaskan panhandle start at the shore. Roads are often carved into the surrounding hills and many streets in town are staircases rather than thoroughfares for auto traffic. Using this to your advantage, you can often get good views of the Narrows, harbor and mountains from the highest points along these streets. Ketchikan's surrounding mountains are a lush green due to the tremendous amount of rainfall in this area. In fact, it's the local populace that has been credited with coining the phrase "liquid sunshine." They also invented the term "Ketchikan Sneakers," referring to the high yellow rubber boots often worn in Alaska. Ketchikaners make fun of the weather by prominently displaying a tall rain gauge outside the Visitors Bureau. Annual rainfall is a staggering 160 inches.

An important note before getting started – in Ketchikan, as in other towns along the Inside Passage, most museums and other tourist attractions have arranged their hours of operation to coincide with cruise ship visits. Therefore we won't mention times when these establishments are open in any of the chapters that follow (except for those ports that are not commonly called at by most cruise ships). We'll also list hours when we believe that there may be a conflict with available shore time.

There's a small but useful information center right at the cruise ship dock and this makes a good place to begin your walking tour. A better place to pick up additional information is at the regional Southeast Alaska Visitor Center located nearby at 50 Main Street. From the dock, cross the busy harborfront street and proceed up Mission Street. Although it's a rather tacky avenue, lined on both sides with souvenir shops, it looks like something from an old western movie that has been mistakenly transported to Alaska. It's amusing in its own way. Mission Street ends at Dock Street, where you should turn to the left and enter the **Tongass Historical Museum**, 629 Dock Street, ☎ (907) 225-5600. Interesting displays will acquaint you with the native Indian tribes and their culture as well as local history. Adult admission is $3.

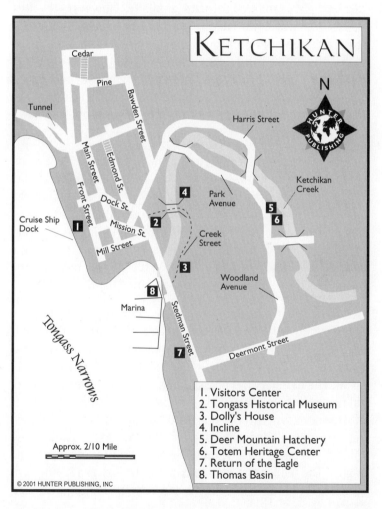

KETCHIKAN

1. Visitors Center
2. Tongass Historical Museum
3. Dolly's House
4. Incline
5. Deer Mountain Hatchery
6. Totem Heritage Center
7. Return of the Eagle
8. Thomas Basin

Approx. 2/10 Mile

© 2001 HUNTER PUBLISHING, INC

After leaving the museum, walk in the opposite direction to Stedman Street and follow the latter for a few blocks until it reaches **Creek Street**. This famous street is actually a boardwalk built on pilings above Ketchikan Creek, like many of the buildings. The city fathers designated Creek Street as the Red Light District in 1903, a status it held for 50 years. Now most of the colorful wooden buildings are restaurants or shops that cater to thousands of tourists annually. However, the first house you will come across on the this street is **"Dolly's House,"** home of Ketchikan's most famous Madam for many years. The house is furnished as it was during the years of her residence and provides an interesting glimpse into Creek Street's very colorful and rowdy past. Be sure to lean over the boardwalk and gaze at both locals and tourists kayaking down Ketchikan Creek.

Adjacent to Creek Street there is a small red incline railway car that for a few cents will take you up the hill to the Westmark Cape Fox Lodge. Spectacular views of the town and harbor can be had on the way up and from the lodge itself. You'll get a bird's-eye view of your own cruise ship and any others that happen to be in port. What is most striking about this picture is how the huge vessels dwarf everything in town – and Ketchikan is one of the larger towns you'll visit!

Leave the Westmark Lodge from the opposite side of the tram and walk down Venetia Avenue into Park Avenue. Turn right and follow Park for a few blocks to the **Deer Mountain Tribal Hatchery & Eagle Center**, 1158 Salmon Road, ☎ (907) 252-5158. The hatchery has fine exhibits describing the varieties of salmon and their unusual life cycle. You can also observe some of the ponds where more than 300,000 salmon are raised each year to ensure adequate supplies. Baked salmon samples are offered. An enclosed area on the grounds contains several bald eagles. The fee for a guided tour of the facility is $7. Adjacent to the Deer Mountain facility is the **Totem Heritage Center**,

601 Deermount Street, ☎ (907) 225-5900. Although it is within the city, the center sits on the edge of Ketchikan's rain forest and has lovely nature trails. It's best known for its collection of authentic 19th-century totem poles (that is, they were not carved for the benefit of the tourists). Local artisans display their carving skills. The adult admission is $2 during the summer and there is no charge on Sundays.

From the Totem Heritage Center return to the waterfront via Deermont Street and then on Stedman, following the harbor. Along the way you'll pass the 70x120-foot **Return of the Eagle** mural, drawn by local artists and representing the renewal of the earth as depicted in Indian belief. A block later is the **Thomas Basin,** the marina where hundreds of boats belonging to Ketchikan's residents are moored. In a place like Ketchikan it's more important to own a boat than a car. In a few blocks you'll be back at the cruise ship dock. The preceding tour, at a leisurely pace, will take about three hours.

All of Ketchikan's major in-town sights are along the route just described. Some organized city tours add on a visit to **Totem Bight State Historic Park,** which is 10 miles north of town. It also has a Tlingit tribal clan house in addition to some totem poles. However, as long as you visit the Totem Heritage Center, or if you're going to be stopping in Sitka where a national historic park offers an outstanding display of totems, don't feel as though you are missing out on anything by touring independently and omitting the state park. Organized shore excursions are better left for a visit to **Saxman Native Village**, about three miles south of Ketchikan. Here you'll observe and learn about the Tlingit, Haida and other Native American cultures. It's a very worthwhile stop for those who are especially interested in learning about these cultures. Should you want to hike or take a cab to the village on your own, admission is free but there's a hefty $30 fee for guided tours. You can do just as well without the guide. A short harbor cruise is another option, but your cruise ship will slowly pass by many of the same sights on its way into and out of Ketchikan, often with narration from onboard staff. In every itinerary either arrival or departure will occur during daylight hours, so you won't miss anything.

Some activities that can't be done on your own or require making reservations onboard your ship include canoe and kayaking trips on Ketchikan Creek and various fishing expeditions. The canoe and kayak trips offer no more in the way of scenery than a walk through town, but they're fun and provide a "get involved" experience. Two interesting excursions are sportfishing trips and a jet boat excursion to beautiful **Salmon Falls.**

Another tour usually available is a combination float plane and boat ride to the nearby **Misty Fjords.** If your cruise ship is one of the few that includes the fjords in its itinerary, then this trip probably won't be offered. (If it is, don't take it because much of it will be a repeat of what you've already seen.) The scenery is beautiful and the experience can be wonderful, but remember that your investment of $200 or more per person may be vitiated by poor visibility and other weather conditions, which are frequently less than ideal.

The amount of time spent in Ketchikan varies considerably from one cruise itinerary to another, but it's usually at least half a day and often closer to a full day. This is more than enough time to explore the city on your own and perhaps take one of the shorter excursions.

For books on the local area, as well as Alaska in general, stop by **Parnassus** at 5 Creek Street, ☎ (907) 225-7690.

Accommodations

Best Western Landing. 3434 Tongass Avenue, ☎ (907) 225-5166 or (800) 528-1234. $$. Modern inn conveniently located across the street from the ferry terminal. Some rooms have gas fireplaces.

Ingersoll Hotel, 303 Mission Street, ☎ (907) 225-2124 or (800) 478-2124. 58 Rooms. $. A historic property in the middle of the downtown area, many units have nice waterfront views. There's a good seafood restaurant on the premises.

Westmark Cape Fox Lodge, 800 Venetia Way, ☎ (907) 225-8001 or (800) 544-0970. 72 Rooms. $$$. Ketchikan's most luxurious accommodations. This attractive lodge sits atop a rocky ledge overlooking the harbor.

Juneau

Juneau, with a population of 30,000, is Alaska's capital city and has so far withstood attempts to move the capital closer to the population center of Anchorage. It has a quaint, small-town atmosphere far different from most American state capital cities. Juneau derives its name from a mid-19th-century gold prospector named Joe Juneau. The city is located snugly at the base of two mountains that tower above the town's buildings on one side and the attractive Gastineau Channel on the other. The setting has been favorably compared to that of a Norwegian fjord. Not far from Juneau is the vast Juneau Ice-field. Residents here are quick to point out that this icecap, the origin of almost 40 separate glaciers, including the famous Mendenhall Glacier, is larger than any found in the Alps and is as big as Switzerland.

There's a lot to see in this very interesting city, which can support its claim as being the heart of the Inside Passage. The cruise ship dock is a few blocks south of downtown and a short walk from here, up Franklin Street, brings you to the **Juneau Library**. An observation deck on the top floor provides outstanding vistas of the Gastineau Channel, Douglas Island and the mountains on the western side of the channel. Continue on Franklin, bearing left after two blocks onto Front Street. This is the center of the downtown shopping district. Notice that most streets are covered to protect residents and visitors from the frequent rain. Many large murals are painted on the sides of buildings, a common feature in towns throughout both the Inside Passage and the Alaskan interior.

Keep to the right on Front Street as it leads into Seward and take the latter for two blocks to Third Street. At the intersection is the **Log Cabin Visitor Center**, where you can pick up brochures and ask any questions you might have about things to see and do in and around town. To the left of the Visitor Center at Third and Main Streets is the **Windfall Fisherman** statue. This beautiful bronze sculpture is a full-size depiction of a brown bear that has just captured a large fish. The statue serves as a dramatic foreground for the **Alaska State Capitol**, which is a block north at Main and Fourth Streets. The structure isn't particularly impressive as state capitols go, but there are some interesting sculptures and paintings on display in the main lobby that show various aspects of Alaskan culture and industry.

Walk around the Seward Street side of the capitol to Fifth Street and turn right, proceeding for two blocks until you reach Gold Street and the **St. Nicholas Orthodox Church**, ☎ (907) 586-1023. Funds from Russia were used to construct this octagon-shaped structure in the 1880s, even though control of Alaska had passed to the Americans more than 20 years earlier. There still was a need to serve the sizable Russian Orthodox community that had developed among the Tlingit Indians. The interior of the church is simple, but filled with many interesting and beautiful icons.

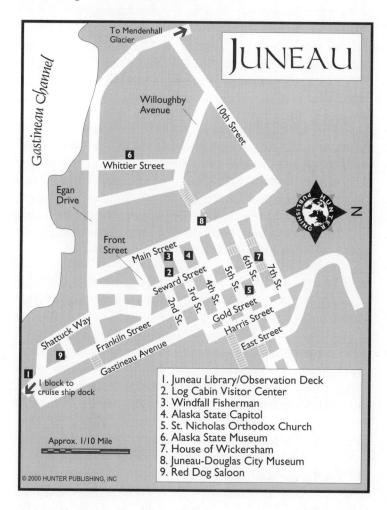

JUNEAU

To Mendenhall Glacier

Gastineau Channel

Willoughby Avenue

10th Street

Whittier Street

Egan Drive

Front Street

Main Street

Seward Street

2nd St.

3rd St.

4th St.

5th St.

6th St.

7th St.

Gold Street

Harris Street

East Street

Shattuck Way

Franklin Street

Gastineau Avenue

1 block to cruise ship dock

Approx. 1/10 Mile

© 2000 HUNTER PUBLISHING, INC

1. Juneau Library/Observation Deck
2. Log Cabin Visitor Center
3. Windfall Fisherman
4. Alaska State Capitol
5. St. Nicholas Orthodox Church
6. Alaska State Museum
7. House of Wickersham
8. Juneau-Douglas City Museum
9. Red Dog Saloon

Having admired the church, head back on Fifth. A little beyond Main Street, Fifth will end at a staircase that leads down a cliff, across a bridge leading through a park-like area and finally to Willoughby Street. (Handicapped individuals can reach the bottom by going to the State Office Building on Fourth Street and taking an elevator.) Proceed on Willoughby for a short distance to Whittier and turn left. You'll soon arrive at the **Alaska State Museum**, 395 Whittier Street, ☎ (907) 465-2901.

This excellent facility, housed in a modern structure, traces the natural and cultural history of the state from prehistoric times to the present in several different galleries. The highlight of the collection is an exhibit featuring a bald eagle nesting in a tree and a brown bear with cub. The two-story exhibit is seen from every side as you ascend or descend a gentle ramp that surrounds it. An 80-foot mural of Alaskan scenery adorns one wall. The admission price is $4 for ages 18 and over.

Once you've completed the Museum, head down Whittier towards the waterfront. At Egan Drive turn left, passing the large Centennial Hall/Forest Service Information Center until you get back to Franklin Street and the dock. This walking tour, including the time spent in the museum, will take close to three hours. If you wish to spend more time in town some other things to explore are the **Juneau-Douglas City Museum**, Fourth & Main Streets, ☎ (907) 586-357 and the **House of Wickersham**, 213 7th Street, ☎ (907) 465-4563. The latter was built for a successful gold-finder in the early 1900s and provides a fine view of the city. You can also visit the grave sites of Joe Juneau and fellow prospector Richard Harris. Finally, there's an excellent fish hatchery, the **Gastineau Salmon Hatchery**, 2697 Channel Drive, ☎ (907) 463-4810. In addition to hatchery operations, there are fish tanks that display more than a hundred species native to Alaska. The admission price is $3, and you can take a guided tour or explore on your own.

An interesting excursion within Juneau is a trip to the top of Mt. Roberts, which offers fantastic panoramic views. For many years the only way to the summit was via a foot trail, but now you can take advantage of the **Mount Roberts Tramway**, 490 S. Franklin Street, ☎ (888) 461-TRAM. The tramway will quickly whisk you to 2,000 feet above the city. In addition to the view, there's a restaurant, gift shop, an interpretive film titled *Seeing Daylight* that describes Tlingit culture, nature center, exhibits on native heritage and hiking trails. If you're lucky, you may even see some wildlife. This can be either a short visit (under a half-hour for the round-trip ride and a few minutes at the top) or can take a couple of hours, allowing you to explore the trails. The fare is approximately $18 for adults. Of course, if you're on a budget you can still hike to the top.

Twelve miles from downtown is the most famous of Juneau's attractions – the **Mendenhall Glacier** (Visitor Center, ☎ 907-789-0097). This is one of the most accessible glaciers in the state and its size is most impressive, despite the fact that it has been receding for the past 250 years! A modern visitor center introduces you to the world of glaciers in general and the Mendenhall in particular. There is an outstanding view of the glacier from the large observation area. (When the center was built in 1962 the edge of the glacier was right outside). An easy ³/₁₀ of a mile paved trail takes you to the best point for viewing and photographing the glacier. Several other trails ranging from a half-mile to almost four miles explore the surrounding area. The glacier itself, seen from across the picturesque Mendenhall Lake, begins 12 miles away in the Juneau Icefield. The front of Mendenhall is 1½ miles across and 100 feet high. You'll see chunks of ice floating in the lake and hear a loud waterfall gushing from Nugget Creek. As this will be the first major glacier for many Alaskan visitors, it's a sight you'll never forget. Chances are that the vivid blue color of

Mendenhall will catch your attention. We must mention here that many visitors are surprised about the "dirty" look of most glaciers, including the Mendenhall. This is not dirt but rather rock and other debris that has been carried and ground up by the moving river of ice in its journey down from the mountains. Alaskans will smile pleasantly at you if you tell them to clean up their glaciers! So avoid the embarrassment and chat with a local about the transportation abilities of glaciers. By the end of this visit you should have a better understanding of how the actions of glaciers affect the landscape.

Many excursions are available in Juneau, including several different tours of the Juneau Icefield and various glaciers. These are generally by float plane and involve a fly-over of the awe-inspiring icefield and, conditions permitting, a stop on the icecap itself. Some include a salmon bake. These tours are the *only way* to see the Juneau Icefield, and thus are among the most worthwhile of all the "flightseeing" trips that you can take while along the Inside Passage. Other interesting diversions are a float trip on the Mendenhall River, a unique way to see the Mendenhall Glacier; and the **Glacier Gardens Rainforest Adventure**. You'll be driven up the slope of pretty Thunder Mountain and pass through botanical gardens and a real Alaskan rain forest. A stop is made at an overlook where you can get a fantastic view of the Mendenhall Valley and the Chilkat Mountains. Should you decide to arrange this tour on your own, it costs $18 and takes about an hour, ☎ (907) 790-3377. There are also fishing expeditions, bus tours to the Glacier (again, some include a salmon bake) and a guided walking trip to the **Lady Lou Revue**, a 90-minute Gay 90s revue in the tradition of shows that entertained the prospectors (but now done in a manner that's suitable for children), ☎ (907) 586-3786. Kayaking and jet boating are also available.

For those wishing to venture out on their own, Juneau also provides that opportunity. Local car rental companies will pick you up at the dock and deliver you back there when you've returned the car. Those driving on their own can take the short ride to the Mendenhall Glacier and explore it at their own pace. The road along the Gastineau Channel continues past the vicinity of Mendenhall and provides scenic views of the Favorite Channel and Auke Bay. This area is known for its frequent whale sightings. A car also comes in handy to cross the bridge onto Douglas Island, a great place to admire the entire surrounding area and home of the **Eaglecrest Ski Area,** ☎ (907) 790-2000.

Time permitting, on the way back into Juneau, stop at the **Gastineau Salmon Hatchery** on Channel Drive off the main road, Egan Drive, ☎ (907) 463-4810. More than 160 million salmon are hatched here every year, including chum, Coho, king, and pink salmon. There are excellent exhibits about the salmon-raising process, as well as a large aquarium with salmon and over 100 other species found in Southeastern Alaskan waters. One more in-town attraction is worth mentioning as a closing thought. Although you'll probably have all of your meals onboard, the **Red Dog Saloon** on Franklin Street just a couple of blocks from the dock is definitely worth a visit, ☎ (907) 463-3777. Stop in for a drink or just to take a look at the odd assortment of "Alaskarama" that covers almost every inch of the walls.

Every cruise ship spends a minimum of six hours in Juneau and most spend considerably more, so you'll always have enough time to do the downtown walking tour and take one or more optional tours, including the must-see Mendenhall Glacier. Whatever you decide, Juneau will provide you with plenty to do and see; it's more likely that you'll run out of time before running out of things to do.

Bookworms can find reading material at either of these two stores: **Big City Books, Ltd.**, 100 N. Franklin, ☎ (907) 586-2130; **Hearthside Books**, 254 Front Street, ☎ (907) 586-1726.

Accommodations

Driftwood Lodge, 435 Willoughby Street, ☎ (907) 586-2280 or (800) 544-2239. 63 rooms. $. Situated close to the Alaska State Museum, the lodge offers regular rooms as well as some with kitchen facilities. Free transportation is provided to and from the ferry terminal.

Goldbelt Hotel Juneau, 51 Egan Drive, ☎ (907) 586-6900 or (888) 478-6909. 105 Rooms. $$$. Features large and unusually attractive guest units. Pleasant waterfront location and excellent restaurant featuring fresh fish and seafood. Public areas are decorated with native arts.

Westmark Baranof, 127 North Franklin Street, ☎ (907) 586-2660 or (800) 544-0970. 196 rooms. $$$. Convenient downtown location within walking distance of most Juneau attractions. Décor ranges from traditional to modern in this historic nine-story structure. Excellent restaurants.

The Lynn Canal, Skagway & Haines

Those of you heading up the Lynn Canal and into Skagway are in for a special treat – some of the Inside Passage's most beautiful scenery and one of its most fascinating ports of call. Skagway is perhaps the quaintest of all stops along the cruise routes and it's a gateway to some remarkable sights, but we're getting a little ahead of ourselves.

The Lynn Canal

The Lynn Canal (again, a natural waterway) is the most northerly of the major navigable portions of the Inside Passage. It begins at the junction of waterways leading south towards the other ports of the Inside Passage and the Icy Strait, which heads westward to Glacier Bay and beyond into the Gulf of Alaska. The canal stretches for 70 miles and measures up to 10 miles wide in some places. It's almost entirely surrounded, like virtually all of the Inside Passage, by the thickly forested mountain slopes of the Tongass National Forest. Nowhere on the Inside Passage, however, are the mountains more beautiful than here. Hundreds of waterfalls add to the picture and you're always within sight of the ice-capped mountain peaks. Few glaciers of significance reach the water here, but they're never very far away.

The Lynn Canal is a remote area with many inlets that you can spot as you cruise along its icy waters. The two major communities are Skagway and Haines. These towns are both on the mainland and are connected by road. However, although they are less than 20 miles apart by boat, you would have to ride for almost 300 miles to get from one to another by car! That tells you something about the mountainous terrain that forms the northern barrier to these communities.

Skagway

This is without a doubt one of the most colorful towns you're likely to visit anywhere. Born in the days of the 1898 Klondike Gold Rush, it was a wild town of over 20,000, populated by prospectors, working girls, gamblers, thieves and criminals of every type. There were more than 80 saloons and probably as many houses of ill repute. Among the most notorious of the town's residents was Jefferson "Soapy" Smith, whose end came in a famous shootout. The excesses of Skagway at the turn of the century can be excused because the prospectors faced an arduous journey over the Klondike. Many would never return and few found the fortune they came to seek. This history is faithfully re-created today in a town that seems to have been left exactly as it was almost a hundred years ago. In fact, the streets are still boardwalks and many of the buildings have false fronts like a movie set. Still the "Gateway to the Klondike," only 825 people live in Skagway at the present time. Most ships that pull into dock at the southern end of town carry more people in passengers and crew than live in Skagway! You'll be pleased to learn that Skagway's location makes its weather considerably better than in other towns of the Inside Passage. Sunshine can almost be considered as common here during the summer months.

Sightseeing within Skagway is remarkably easy because the entire town is five blocks wide and about 25 blocks long. From the cruise ship dock at the head of the Lynn Canal, cross the tracks of the White Pass & Yukon Railway (more about this later) and reach 1st Street. Go right one block to Broadway, the town's principal thoroughfare and the area where most attractions are concentrated. Your first stop should be the **Klondike Gold Rush National Historic Park Visitor Center**, Broadway and 2nd Street, ☎ (907) 983-2921. Almost the entire town and some scenic areas to the north are part of the park. (So, too, is an area to the south of downtown Seattle, Washington, the other end of the Klondike Gold Rush story.) The Visitor Center will provide you with a good understanding of the tumultuous Gold Rush era. Brochures describing many of the historic buildings on Broadway are available here. As you walk along the boardwalks (cars ride along semi-paved or dirt streets) you'll feel as if you have traveled back in time. The colorful buildings have been faithfully restored to their original appearance. Probably the most famous structure in town (and certainly the most photographed) is the **Arctic Brotherhood**

Hall, Broadway between 2nd and 3rd Streets. The front of the building is faced with more than 20,000 pieces of driftwood that were gathered from nearby beaches. The **Trail of '98 Museum**, ☎ (907) 983-2420, was recently relocated to inside the Brotherhood Hall and contains interesting artifacts and exhibits dealing with the Gold Rush era. The adult admission price is $2.

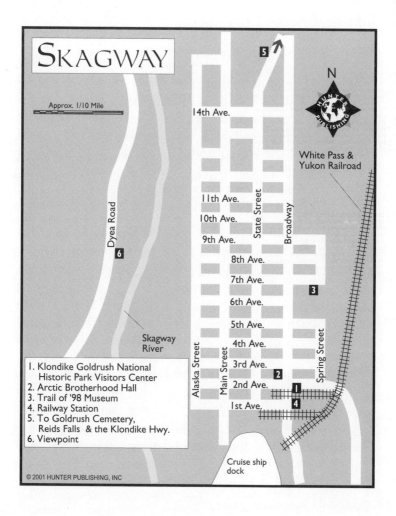

SKAGWAY

Approx. 1/10 Mile

N

HUNTER PUBLISHING

14th Ave.

White Pass & Yukon Railroad

11th Ave.
10th Ave.
9th Ave.
8th Ave.
7th Ave.
6th Ave.
5th Ave.
4th Ave.
3rd Ave.
2nd Ave.
1st Ave.

State Street
Broadway
Alaska Street
Main Street
Spring Street

Dyea Road

Skagway River

1. Klondike Goldrush National
   Historic Park Visitors Center
2. Arctic Brotherhood Hall
3. Trail of '98 Museum
4. Railway Station
5. To Goldrush Cemetery,
   Reids Falls & the Klondike Hwy.
6. Viewpoint

Cruise ship dock

© 2001 HUNTER PUBLISHING, INC

Ports of Call

Other reminders of the past range from turn-of-the-century buses and taxis (that you can ride) to the second floor of many of the town's saloons (now restaurants or pubs). Peering out from the windows are mannequins of seductively clad "painted ladies," encouraging the prospectors to come up for a visit. Candles behind a red glass cover burn throughout the day to let you know what used to occupy these premises.

It's little things like these and the dummy gold-panning prospector sitting on a bench that add authenticity to the Gold Rush-era atmosphere that permeates Skagway.

Entertaining performances are provided throughout the summer at the **Days of '98 Show With Soapy Smith**, in the Eagle's Hall at Broadway and 6th Street. This is one of the most popular attractions for visitors to Skagway and is a part of many optional shore excursions. You can also see it on your own (show times are at 10:30 am, 2:00 pm and 8:00 pm, so there should be a performance that coincides with the time your ship is in port). Tickets cost $12-14 for adults, with the higher price being for the evening show.

Half a mile north of town (via State Street following signs) is the **Gold Rush Cemetery**. Here, amid a graveyard that will remind you of a scene from a horror-film spoof, are the remains of the town's famous and infamous residents. These include "Soapy" Smith and Frank Reid, the unfortunate man selected by the townspeople to bring Smith to justice. Both died in a gunfight more famous in Alaska than the shootout at the O.K. Corral. Much of the cemetery is in a state of chaos, the graves not generally being attended to, but that too adds to ambiance of your visit. A short trail leads from behind the cemetery to **Reid's Falls**. It's hidden from view when you're in the cemetery, but just follow the sound of its rushing waters and you can't miss it.

The town of Skagway is so small that, except for time devoted to browsing through the many shops (including souvenir places too numerous to count), you can cover just about everything in well under two hours, not counting the time for the Days of '98 Show. That will leave you with plenty of time to explore the many areas of scenic beauty that lie beyond Skagway, either on your own or by escorted tours. The White Pass & Yukon Railroad is the primary attraction, and we'll profile it last. Among other tours are the combined flying/floating trip to the **Haines Bald Eagle Preserve** and **Glacier Bay Flightseeing**. The former is an interesting excursion and you're almost sure to sight the elusive bald eagle on this trip. The latter is a good idea only if your cruise does not actually sail into Glacier Bay. Although the perspective of Glacier Bay from the air is spectacular, the time (and money) it requires may not be worth it if your cruise itinerary covers it.

Now it's time for the Skagway highlight – **The White Pass & Yukon Railroad**. Its depot is at Broadway and 2nd Street, ☎ (800) 343-7373 or (907) 983-2217. Excursions travel over the line that was built in 1900 to transport prospectors on the first leg of their journey to the Klondike region. The trip is a lot more comfortable today, but you'll be seeing much the same things the prospectors did – a narrow river valley surrounded by towering mountains on either side, the gorge being filled with wonderful waterfalls. The train carries you over "frightening" wooden trestles, through tunnels and over deep and very narrow ravines, and is one of the most scenic train rides in all of North America.

While no one who takes this exciting excursion is likely to be disappointed, it still isn't, in our opinion, the best way to see the area. It travels only as far as the White Pass (the border with Canada), where you have the option to continue into the Yukon via motor coach. The trip costs about $78 per adult and you will find that renting a car in Skagway and taking the 130-

mile round-trip journey to Carcross in the Yukon Territory is less expensive and just as worthwhile. (Depending upon how much time you have, you might even be able to travel the additional 65 miles round trip to the capital of the Yukon, Whitehorse.) If you select this option, your trip begins at the north end of Skagway where the **Klondike Highway** begins. The most scenic portion of this route is between Skagway and Carcross. The first 14 miles (to the Canadian border) are on the opposite side of the gorge that the railroad travels on. There are several overlooks on this well-paved and maintained road that offer a chance to admire the scenery and to watch the trains going by.

Once you've entered the Yukon, the road traverses an area that resembles a moonscape before reaching a beautiful mountain wilderness with green glacial lakes, towering peaks, and gloriously colorful wildflowers. Again, there are pull-outs at some of the most scenic spots. The town of Carcross isn't very much to look at, but it does have a couple of interesting attractions and is also a good place for lunch (this excursion will require having lunch away from your ship). The **Carcross Desert**, just north of town, is reputedly the world's smallest and signs explain why this desert developed in a region that is usually a lush green from considerable rainfall. **Frontierland**, just north of town on the Klondike Highway, is a re-created town that will be of interest to children, and the adjacent **Yukon Museum of Natural History**, ☎ (867) 821-4055, has excellent stuffed specimens of bears and other large animals native to the area. The surrounding grounds cover 30 acres containing native animals and plants as well as splendid views of Lake Bennett and the surrounding mountains. The combined admission is $6.50 (Canadian) or you can visit either attraction alone for $4.

Being able to go beyond the White Pass is only one advantage of having a car in Skagway. Once you get back to Skagway you can also cross the bridge at the north end of town that leads to Dyea Road. At the end of this road, nine miles farther, is the beginning of the Chilkoot Trail, a three-day hike into the Yukon. As a cruise ship passenger you won't be doing the trail (unless you want to miss the boat) but there are several places along Dyea Road where you can stop for panoramic views of the town, the docks and snowcapped mountains in every direction. You can also drive to the Gold Rush Cemetery and Reid's Falls instead of taking a long walk or using public transportation. In any event, allow about four hours for the complete round-trip excursion to Carcross. (Note that car rental companies in Skagway may change from time to time, so those who plan on renting should contact the Skagway Visitors Bureau for information. See *Addenda*, page 199.)

Other tour options include horseback riding, kayak and jet boat rips and wildlife tours. Kayaks, which we've already encountered at the previous ports of call, are worth mentioning because they are a good means of exploring and having fun for people who aren't experienced boaters. Kayaks are extremely stable and are easy to paddle.

Since most vessels going to Skagway allow at least six hours in port, there is plenty of time to see everything in town and take a Yukon excursion either by train or car. All shore excursions in Skagway are long enough to do the White Pass & Yukon Railroad and some additional sightseeing. If you're going to the Yukon, however, there won't be time for other tours unless your ship is scheduled to spend a minimum of eight hours here.

Accommodations

Skagway Inn Bed & Breakfast, 7th Avenue & Broadway, ☎ (907) 983-2289. 12 rooms. $$. This attractive and interesting little inn was, not surprisingly, a bordello during the wild gold rush days. It features comfortable furnishings and a friendly staff. A bountiful full breakfast is included in the room rate.

Westmark Inn, 3rd & Spring Streets, ☎ (907) 983-6000 or (800) 544-0970. 220 rooms. $$. The rather small rooms and mediocre décor probably helps to explain why this is one of the lowest-priced members of the usually prestigious Westmark family. Still, it's the biggest place in town and the best, too, which says something about the quality of accommodations in Skagway.

Haines

Not many cruise ships make a stop at Haines, which is unfortunate because its setting is every bit as beautiful as that of Skagway. On a small peninsula formed by the Chilkat River and the Lynn Canal, Haines affords vistas of not only the canal, but the coastal mountains as well. The town was established in 1879 as a mission to convert the natives to Christianity, but it wasn't long before it became the trailhead for an alternative route to the Klondike. For a short time there was even some gold mining very close to the town itself.

You can begin a brief walking tour of downtown at the Visitor Center on 2nd and Willard. Nearby is the **Sheldon Museum**, Main Street at 2nd Avenue, ☎ (907) 766-2366, which should not be confused with the Sheldon Jackson Museum in Sitka. The museum contains an impressive collection of native artifacts as well as exhibits pertaining to the history of the Haines area. The other in-town point of interest is the remains of **Fort William Henry Seward,** located at the south end of town, ☎ (907) 766-2234. Of noted interest are the attractions centered around the former Parade Ground.

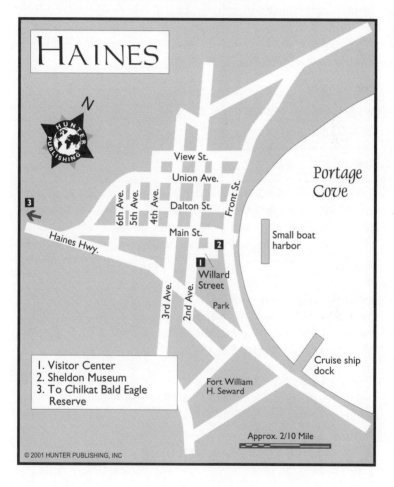

Here you'll find an authentic Chilkat Indian tribal house, a log cabin typical of the pioneer days and several totem poles. Native Americans also demonstrate their carving skills within the grounds of the fort. A performing arts center on the grounds is home to the **Chilkat Indian Dances**. Native Americans perform Tlingit dances in colorful costumes. A 45-minute-long performance is given Sunday through Thursday at either 7:30 or 8:30 pm (check locally for times). The admission is $10 for adults.

The Haines Highway heads north out of town and links up with the Alaska Highway some 150 miles away. Cruise passengers obviously won't have time to get that far if you rent a car, but there is beautiful scenery en route and a lot closer to town.

Pull-outs near Mileposts 6 and 9 will give you a better look at the Chilkat River and the lofty Takhinsha Mountains that form the town's northern barrier. Ten miles farther is a pull-out for the **Chilkat Bald Eagle Preserve**. While the greatest concentration of these magnificent creatures (sometimes as many as 4,000) occurs in October through early winter, you're almost certain to sight quite a few here during the summer. Moose, bear and other wildlife are also very common year-round. Finally, if you're here in mid-August, you can spend some time at the colorful five-day **Southeast Alaska State Fair**.

Whether you arrive by cruise ship or the ferry you should consider one of several tours that visit the Chilkat Bald Eagle Preserve or take a ride on Chilkoot Lake. If you're on your own in Haines, stop into the Visitor Center for information on the available tours. Prices range from $40-60.

Accommodations

Eagle's Nest Motel, 1069 Haines Highway, ☎ (907) 766-2891. 13 rooms. $. Basic accommodations, which is about all you can expect in Haines, especially in the lower-price category. The rooms are clean and comfortable and the surrounding scenery is fine.

Captain's Choice Motel, 108 2nd Avenue, ☎ (907) 766-3111. 39 Rooms. $$. Attractive rustic rooms overlooking pleasant scenery. Free transportation to the ferry terminal is provided.

Glacier Bay National Park

We encountered our first glaciers in a previous chapter and learned some interesting facts about them. Glacier Bay is a unique National Park. It offers Alaska's and perhaps the world's greatest concentration of tidewater glaciers compressed into a relatively small area. There are 16 tidewater glaciers contained within the bay, most of which will be at least partially visible on your visit. The bay's glaciers are among the most rapidly retreating in all of Alaska. Glacier Bay is now about 65 miles long and was at one time totally covered by ice. The retreating process could stop next year or it could go on for hundreds of years. The best scientists in the field cannot predict when such a change will occur, if at all. You will encounter many glaciers that are advancing as we continue our Alaska cruise.

As your ship enters Glacier Bay, a launch from the National Park Service will pull up alongside and a couple of Park Rangers will come on board to provide commentary, answer questions and distribute literature.

Glacier Bay is surrounded by the mighty Fairweather Mountain Range, which provides all of the snow necessary to have created the many glaciers that envelop three sides of the horseshoe-shaped bay. These same mountains provide a magnificent backdrop to the glaciers, a dozen of which are currently calving icebergs into the bay. The term "calving" vividly portrays the process by which the glaciers "give birth" to icebergs. **Johns Hopkins Glacier** is the highlight of those found here. Originating more than 11 miles back into the mountains, the glacier is 45 miles from the beginning of the bay. It's so active that ships are generally kept two miles from its face to avoid getting in the way of newly created icebergs that fall from its 200-foot wall of ice. "White Thunder" is the term given to the deafening noise made as they crash into the water below. Even from two miles away, John Hopkins is an impressive sight that you'll be sure to remember. At certain times of the year, notably in June, access to the area of Johns Hopkins or other portions of the Bay may be partially restricted so as not to interfere with the birth of seal pups.

Among other glaciers that can be seen from the deck of your ship are Reid, Lamplugh, Grand and Brady, all originating from the massive Brady Icefield on the bay's western side. Because of the active nature of the glaciers, the waters that you'll be cruising on are literally filled with thousands of icebergs, some already melted down to the size of a small rock, while others are still quite enormous. Even smaller ones are larger than they appear – only one-sixth of the total surface of an iceberg stays above the water. You'll enjoy standing by the deck railing as your ship cuts through the thinner parts of the ice floes, often making a crunching sound not that different from the noise your car makes as it crushes ice beneath its wheels.

Although Glacier Bay contains many beautiful glaciers, there are even bigger and more magnificent ones to be seen in other portions of your cruise. However, few places can match this area for the opportunity to see examples of Alaska's abundant bird population, seals, otters and whales.

Let's talk about the birds first. There are several types of birds that make the cliffs of ice in Glacier Bay their summer home. Tens of thousands congregate here in large groups. As your ship approaches the glaciers the noise from such a great number of birds can be quite loud and the sight of hundreds of them fluttering about, with even more resting in the rock crevices and on ledges, is quite a spectacle. It would be worth the trip even if there were no glaciers to be seen! If you're lucky, you might catch a glimpse of the colorful Alaska puffin, although they are more likely to be seen in other, more remote portions of the state.

Hundreds of brown seals live in the waters of Glacier Bay and they love to lie around on icebergs, especially if there is some sunshine. From a distance you are not even aware of their presence, as all you see are small dark spots on the floating icebergs. Someone with binoculars and sharp eyes will soon yell "They're seals!" and all realize it a moment later. Often seals will ignore the presence of the huge ship, but at other times will dive into the water. Sea otters are not as common as seals, but your Park Service hosts will probably point some out to you.

Everyone who goes to Alaska hopes to see some whales, and you're most likely to spot them near the entrance of Glacier Bay. If your captain is especially kind (and they usually are), he'll stop the ship for a time if there are any whales to be seen.

The two types of whales most common in these waters are the orca, or killer whale, and the humpback, with the latter being the most populous. Orcas average 20 to 25 feet and are easily recognizable by their six-foot-high dorsal fin. The larger humpbacks measure between 40 and 50 feet. These social animals are usually in large groups. Sometimes you will just see the tops of their huge bodies protruding above the water's surface. But often they can put on quite a show, rolling over on their sides, expelling water from their blow holes, and the most spectacular sight of all – breaching, when almost their entire body surges out of the water for a brief moment. Seconds later, only their graceful tails are visible above the surface.

A majority of visitors to Glacier Bay will see quite a bit of wildlife. Don't be too disappointed if you don't spot a whale, bald eagle or seal on the first day – there will be plenty of other opportunities.

Your visit to Glacier Bay ends as it began, with the arrival of the Park Service launch, this time to take the Rangers back to their headquarters in the nearby but extremely isolated settlement of Gustavus. Four or more hours are generally spent within the bay, and the ever-changing panorama of mountains, snow, ice, water and wildlife will have made the time fly rapidly by.

> Comment: Because of restrictions on the number of ships allowed into Glacier Bay at any one time, a number of cruises do omit it. We think a cruise without Glacier Bay misses a very special place.

Sitka

One of the more attractive communities in Southeast Alaska, Sitka has always been of strategic importance due to its location, which provides access not only to the Inside Passage, but the Pacific Ocean as well. It was for this reason that the Russians chose Sitka as the capital of their Alaskan settlement and it brought them into conflict with the local natives – the Tlingits. More about this when we get to Sitka National Historic Park. Even today Sitka preserves the greatest evidence of Russian influence of any place in Alaska and the Native American input is also felt strongly here.

Set amid a maze of hundreds of islands surrounded by mountains, Sitka is home to about 8,700 people and is a charming and interesting place to visit. It's a worthwhile part of any cruise that stops there. No cruise ships can dock in town – all ships weigh anchor in the sizable harbor and passengers are brought to shore by tender. Once on the dock though, you're in the heart of everything there is to see.

Adjacent to the boat dock is the **Centennial Building** and **Isabel Miller Museum**, ☎ (907) 747-6455. The large Centennial Building is the scene of many events in town, including the ever-popular performances by colorfully dressed Russian Dancers. Show times generally coincide with ship visits and can best be seen as part of pre-arranged tours, which will be discussed a little later. The museum focuses on local history, including the Native population.

A short walk to the north of the Centennial Building on Harbor Drive is the town square (actually a circle) in the middle of which is **St. Michael's Cathedral**. This beautiful domed structure was built in 1966 to replace the original church, which dated from 1848 and was destroyed by a fire. It is the foremost example of Russian church architecture in North America. A large number of Tlingits are still members of the Orthodox congregation and the cathedral houses numerous beautiful icons and religious artifacts.

Continue west on Lincoln Street, Sitka's main thoroughfare, which is lined with shops of every type. Soon you'll reach a staircase that will take you to **Castle Hill**, location of the stately home of Alexander Baranov, head of the Russian-American Trading Company that ruled Alaska for so many years. It was here that the transfer of sovereignty from Russia to the United States took place after Seward's purchase of the Alaska Territory. Although the castle itself is long gone, the site contains numerous cannons and flags that represent the nations that have ruled over Alaska. Its prime hilltop setting affords visitors a beautiful view of the entire Sitka area, including Mt. Edgecumbe, a 3,000-foot high volcanic mountain. At the base of Castle Hill on the north side of Lincoln Street is the **Sitka Pioneer Home**. Established in 1913 to house aging "sourdoughs" (individuals who came to Alaska to find their fortune and were now 'veterans' of Alaska), the large building is still home to a number of people. A large statue commemorates the prospectors on the spacious and attractive front lawn of the home. Just a block or so north of here are the remains of a large Russian fort. Only one of the wooden blockhouses is still intact.

After you've finished with these downtown attractions, proceed in the other direction on Lincoln Street, going past the cathedral until you reach the **Russian Bishop's House**. This is now part of the Sitka National Historic Park. The building is the largest remaining Russian-built structure in Alaska and has been nicely restored to its appearance of the 1850s. At that time it was home to the influential Bishop of the Russian Orthodox Church in Alaska. Exhibits explain the role of the church in Sitka's Russian days. You can observe the original walls and foundations in some rooms and learn about the restoration process that has been taking place here. The admission price is $3. Continue on the same street and you'll come to the campus of Sheldon Jackson College and the well-known **Sheldon Jackson Museum**, 104 College Drive, ☎ (907) 747-

898l. This museum, housed in a large and modern circular building, is one of the most comprehensive collections of artifacts and exhibits devoted solely to the history and culture of Alaska's native peoples, including the Eskimo, Aleut, Haida, Tlingit and Athabascan cultures. The admission price is $3 for those 18 years and older.

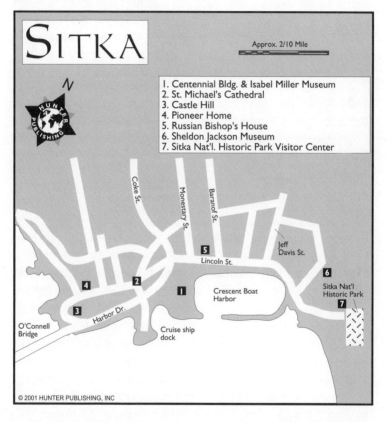

Just a short walk past the museum is the Visitor Center and entrance to the main section of **Sitka National Historic Park**. Situated about a mile's walk from the tender docking area, the lovely and now serene park documents the battle fought between the Russians and Tlingits for control of the area. With the Russian victory, the Tlingits no longer presented a threat to Russian domination of Alaska. What makes the park most attractive, though, is its nearly two miles of well maintained pathways through lush wooded areas. Scattered along the main walk (with a few more at the Visitor Center) are a total of 28 colorful totem poles. Their location amid the tranquil forest significantly enhances their appeal. The ones currently on display are exact replicas of the original carvings that are now falling apart. Although the totems represent various native groups from almost every part of Southeastern Alaska, with the majority being from the Tlingit or Haida cultures, curiously none of them came from the Sitka area itself.

By reversing your route, you will pass Crescent Harbor as you head back to the tender. This is where hundreds of private boats tie up when they're not out on the many waterways that surround the town.

A walking tour of Sitka as described above will take approximately 2½ to 3 hours. The range of optional tours in Sitka is not as great as in other ports of call, but some are very interesting and should be included with your visit. Renting a car in Sitka is not necessary or desirable because everything that should be seen (and can be visited on your own) is close by. Fishing trips are always popular, as are a variety of marine wildlife cruises that ply the waters between the many islands in Sitka's vicinity. Another optional tour along these lines is the cruise to **Silver Bay**. While this one doesn't highlight wildlife, you'll still see many birds and animals along the shoreline. The trip passes by mile after mile of logs awaiting transportation to the Lower 48 and elsewhere, as well as historic mines and other relics of Sitka's past.

We previously mentioned the **Russian Dancers** at the Centennial Building. Tours that take in these lively and entertaining performers usually include some town sightseeing as well. Since not every ship arrival coincides with performances, this may not be offered on your cruise, but if it is, you should book in advance. Those with more time in Sitka who wish to make advance reservations can call ☎ (907) 747-6774 or 688-0880.

Sitka port calls last between four and eight hours depending upon the ship. There's always time to do the walking tour and usually take in an optional tour or two. **Old Harbor Books** at 201 Lincoln, ☎ (907-747-8808) is an excellent place to pick up extra reading material.

Accommodations

Mountain View Bed & Breakfast, 201 Cascade Creek Road, ☎ (907) 747-8966. 5 Rooms. $. For the price you'll get a comfortable and attractive room that sits atop a pretty hill and overlooks the ocean. Our only complaint is that the breakfast is kind of sparse for a B&B.

Westmark Shee Atika, 330 Seward Street, ☎ (907) 747-6241 or (800) 544-0970. 101 rooms. $$. Full-service facility with dining and entertainment on the premises. Attractive and modern rooms, most of which offer excellent mountain or harbor views.

Wrangell

This community of about 2,500 hearty, rather independent souls is not one of the more common stops for cruise ships. In some ways that's an advantage because there is far less commercialization here than in any other sizable town on the Inside Passage. Wrangell has always been and remains primarily a fishing and lumbering town. There are few adjustments that have been made to accommodate the tourist trade.

Located on the scenic Zimovia Strait, Wrangell has a strong Russian influence dating back to its founding in 1834. You'll probably come into town by ship's tender and, as everything in town is with a short distance of the dock, you'll have no trouble getting around. Wrangell's Visitor Center is set in a hut close to the dock on Outer Drive. Then take 2nd Street to visit the **Wrangell Museum**, in the Community Center at the corner of Church Street, ☎ (907) 874-3770. It was built in 1906 and once served as the town's first schoolhouse. Now it chronicles Wrangell's history through exhibits and artifacts. The adult admission price is $2. Note the totem poles in front of the adjacent Public Library building, the first of many that you'll encounter throughout Wrangell.

Walk down Front Street past the Visitor Center until you come upon **Kiksadi Totem Park**. The poles were placed here in 1987 by one of the several Alaskan Native corporations that have been established throughout the state to help preserve traditional Native American cultures while fostering economic development.

Front Street will lead into Shakes Street and end after crossing a bridge onto **Chief Shakes Island**, set in the middle of Inner Boat Harbor. On the way you'll pass some of Wrangell's active canneries, as well as a former pulp mill. Here you'll find even more totem poles, but the primary attraction is the **Shakes Community House**, a community center that displays various items made by the tribe. There is also an excellent view of the harbor from this point. The island is named for a former tribal chieftain whose grave site is back across the bridge on Cass Avenue. Note the two totem poles depicting killer whales that stand guard at the entrance.

Port calls in Wrangell aren't that long but will be enough to cover the approximately two hours needed to see the sights in town and perhaps take a short optional tour. Most of these tours involve cruises that navigate the narrow passages between many islands. Fishing expeditions are also a very popular activity. While none of them can be termed spectacular they are, nonetheless, pleasant ways to spend a few hours in and around the town of Wrangell.

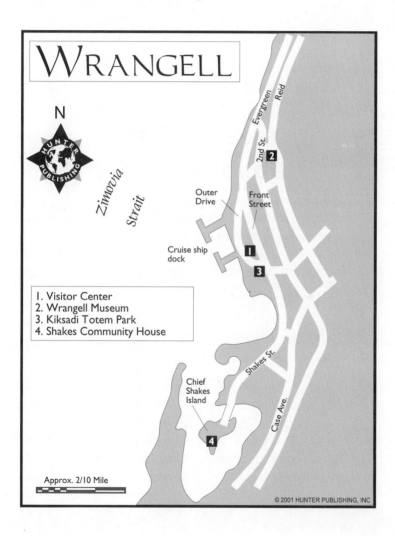

1. Visitor Center
2. Wrangell Museum
3. Kiksadi Totem Park
4. Shakes Community House

Approx. 2/10 Mile

© 2001 HUNTER PUBLISHING, INC

Accommodations

Stikine Inn, City Dock (two blocks from the ferry terminal), ☎ (907) 874-3388. 33 rooms. $. Pickings are slim in Wrangell, but this place will do nicely as it's located close to the attractions and the ferry terminal. There is a restaurant on the premises.

Yakutat Bay, Hubbard Glacier

Beautiful Yakutat Bay forms a deep indentation in the coast of Alaska just north of the town of the same name. This is where the panhandle of Southeastern Alaska ends and the south central coast area of the Gulf of Alaska begins. The bay is surrounded by some of the biggest mountains of the entire Coastal Range, including 18,114-foot-high Mt. Elias. Many of the peaks are within the rugged and largely inaccessible Wrangell-St. Elias National Park. Aside from visits by the most adventurous wilderness hikers and explorers, your cruise ship provides the only other practical way to see at least a part of this huge park.

As you cruise around Yakutat Bay you'll see many glaciers, including Malaspina Glacier at the western edge and Turner Glacier. However, the highlight of any trip here is a close-up visit to the magnificent Hubbard Glacier. In the mid-1980s this was one of the most rapidly advancing glaciers in Alaska. In fact, one of the fjords in the bay was turned into a lake when it was cut off from Yakutat by the advancing wall of ice. A portion of the wall has since broken off, once again opening up the fjord.

Despite occasional brief retreats, Hubbard is still advancing and is one of Alaska's more active glaciers. This is probably your best chance to see the process of calving – blocks of ice falling from the edge of the glacier into the water. Often you'll hear the grinding and crunching sound of ice before it actually breaks off. Note the waves that form when a large piece of ice hits the water. It's a dramatic sight that you'll never forget and one that thrills again and again, no matter how many times you see it. In areas like Hubbard Glacier you'll probably see this happen quite often.

As you admire this natural wonder from the comfort of your ship at the face of the glacier (the face, by the way, is the name given to the very front of the wall of ice), take notice of its many different features. You'll see deep fissures and cracks within the ice, some of which are so large they appear like a rocky mountain cave entrance. Another beautiful feature of this and other large glaciers is the fantastic array of shapes taken by the ice at the very top of the glacier. They appear as pinnacles, arches and other forms similar to the unusual eroded land masses in America's Southwest. The only difference is that these being ice, they constantly vary. Today's pinnacle might be a floating iceberg tomorrow, though there are sure to be new forms to take its place.

Some statistics about this gorgeous hunk of ice are in order. The face of the glacier is more than six miles across, of which a three-mile section is visible from the deck of your ship. It is approximately 300 feet high and dwarfs even the largest of cruise ships. The river of ice that is Hubbard Glacier originates 92 miles away, making it the largest glacier in North America.

Glaciers are like any other beautiful scenery in that you'll never tire of seeing more of them. But no matter how many you encounter, Hubbard, as one of Alaska's most spectacular sights, stands a strong chance of being at or near the top of your list of favorites.

Prince William Sound, College Fjord, Columbia Glacier

Prince William Sound, like Southeastern Alaska, is a world of mountains, fjords, beautiful coastline and glaciers. It leads directly into the open sea, unlike the Inside Passage, and contains many islands and narrow inlets. The 15,000-square-mile Sound is bordered by the high mountains of the Kenai and Chugach Ranges. The magnificent coastal mountain scenery alone would be enough to make a memorable visit to the brilliant blue waters of Prince William Sound, but the very best sights are the stunning glaciers and fjords in the Sound's northern reaches. Those who'll be visiting Valdez (described in the next section) will be spending more time cruising through this area as it is tucked away in the Sound's most northeastern corner.

Having passed mile after glorious mile of icebergs laden with sunning seals, your ship will approach the huge **Columbia Glacier**. If the weather is not cooperative the seals will not be as plentiful, but they'll probably still be around, so watch carefully. Columbia Glacier is another 300-foot-high wall of ice that stretches for almost three miles across the face. It's been receding rapidly in recent years, but it's still massive enough to make a lasting impression. Your ship might get to within a mile of the face and at that distance you'll have an opportunity to witness calving to almost rival that encountered at Hubbard.

Spectacular **College Fjord** contains no fewer than 26 separate glaciers, each named for an eastern college (mainly Ivy League) that supported an exploratory expedition of this area. Harvard Glacier is the most famous of the College Fjord's members and is the one most cruise ships choose to stop at and admire. The area also abounds with wildlife and you'll most likely see one or more bird rookeries as you cruise by. College Fjord's beauty is renowned not only for the many glaciers, but for the majestic mountains, which hem in the fjord and set it off from the rest of Prince William Sound. Take some time to gaze at the view. You'll see miles of mountains with a series of silver ribbons – the glaciers – dropping precipitously from them and finally reaching the icy waters of the fjord. It's not uncommon to see as many as six or seven major glaciers lining your route at one time. The view is simply spectacular in any weather – it ranges from an eerie type of beauty that is present on cloudy days to one of brilliant colors in the sunshine – and often can change during the time you spend here. Sometimes thin bands of clouds hang across the upper or middle portions of the mountains and provide a vivid contrast to the lush green vegetation that clings to them, framed at both top and bottom by the beautiful blue of the sky and sea.

We've been so busy setting the stage for your visit to the fjord that we've neglected the glaciers a bit. Harvard is 340 feet high at the center and is 1½ miles wide. It is bordered by velvety green mountains on either side. Harvard is an excellent example of how rocks form those "dirty" lines in the glacier. The sides of Harvard are filled with debris – a classic moraine. The middle section is almost entirely clear and is a vivid blue.

Among other major active glaciers in College Ford are Yale, which is retreating, and Wellesley. The latter is advancing fairly rapidly but not at the same pace that saw it advance more than 600 feet in the period from 1981 through 1986. One interesting social note on College Fjord – it seems that the people who gave the names to the various glaciers were very concerned with proper etiquette. Since most of the schools for which the glaciers are named were not co-ed at the time, all of the glaciers named after women's colleges are on one side of the fjord. while the men's are on the other side. However, don't take this matter of treating glaciers as if they're living things too far. There isn't any such thing as a male or female glacier!

Valdez

Valdez conjures up visions of the Alaska Pipeline, oil spills and other negatives in the minds of many people. That's unfortunate, because a visit to Valdez is a rewarding experience. Located in a beautiful setting on Valdez Bay, an extension of Prince William Sound, Valdez has earned the title of "Switzerland of America." Ringed by snow-capped peaks, the alpine environment is quite appealing.

Three events have shaped the history of Valdez – gold, an earthquake and oil. The town began like so many others in Alaska as a mining community. It remained a small town, largely dependent on fishing for many years until the 1964 Easter earthquake came and totally destroyed Valdez. Rather than rebuild where the town had been, it was decided to construct a new town some four miles away on ground that was geologically safer. The current status of Valdez came into focus with its selection as the southern terminus of the Alaska Pipeline, an 800-mile-long engineering masterpiece that ranks with the greatest construction projects in history.

Despite the vast size of the pipeline terminal complex, Valdez itself remains a small and rather drab-looking community. You can walk into town from the ship docking point, although you might prefer to make use of the bus service provided by the town and cruise lines. There isn't that much to see within the town itself, although tours of the US Coast Guard's **Vessel Traffic Center**, a block west of the Small Boat Harbor on Clifton Avenue, are of interest.

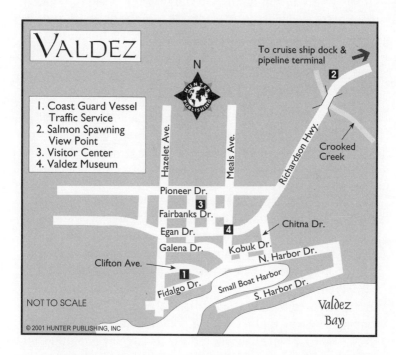

VALDEZ

N

To cruise ship dock & pipeline terminal

1. Coast Guard Vessel Traffic Service
2. Salmon Spawning View Point
3. Visitor Center
4. Valdez Museum

Hazelet Ave.
Meals Ave.
Richardson Hwy.
Crooked Creek

Pioneer Dr.
Fairbanks Dr.
Egan Dr.
Chitna Dr.
Galena Dr.
Kobuk Dr.
N. Harbor Dr.
Clifton Ave.
Fidalgo Dr.
Small Boat Harbor
S. Harbor Dr.

Valdez Bay

NOT TO SCALE

© 2001 HUNTER PUBLISHING, INC

The **Valdez Museum**, 217 Egan Drive, ☎ (907) 835-2764, has local history exhibits highlighting the life of a pioneer gold seeker and the building of the oil pipeline. Pictures of Valdez both before and after the devastating 1964 earthquake are also of interest, as are the model of the pipeline terminal and an exhibit on the clean-up of the *Exxon Valdez* spill. The adult admission is $3. Several fish hatcheries and processing plants are open to the public.

Perhaps the most fascinating attraction within town is the **Salmon Spawning View Point** over the Crooked Creek on Richardson Highway about a half-mile northeast of the town center. During July and August the creek is often so crowded with salmon desperately attempting to make their way upstream that you can hardly see the water! It's sad to see that many actually die in the attempt. Most of the optional tours in Valdez make a brief stop here, but if you're visiting during the spawning season make a point to visit this spot. It would be hard to find any other place where this act of nature can be seen so vividly.

It would be worth taking a cruise that included Valdez just to see the superb setting. However, numerous optional tours available to cruise ship passengers make it one of the finest destinations. Optional tours are the way to go at this port.

The tour of the **Alyeska Pipeline Service Company** oil terminal is certainly one of the most popular area attractions. It can be visited only by organized tour, ☎ (907) 835-2686. Everyone has to get off the bus at the gate and go through a security inspection before being granted admission. A competent guide explains the entire process of how oil is transported to Valdez, how it is stored, and the process of loading it onto tankers for shipment. The bus tour route passes by four berths where tankers as large as 265,000 tons tie up to take on their precious cargo. It then climbs to a hilltop location where you can see many of the 18 oil storage tanks close up. Each is 250 feet in diameter and 62 feet high, and capable of holding up to 510,000 barrels of oil. That's over 21 million gallons! If you drove 20,000 miles a year at 20 miles per gallon it would take more than 20,000 years to empty one of the storage tanks. There is a brief stop at an exhibit area, which depicts the operations of the terminal. From this vantage point there is an outstanding view of the entire terminal complex as well as Valdez Bay, the town, and its surrounding mountains. Because this attraction can only be seen by tour it is a popular shore excursion with cruise passengers. However, you can also join tours that depart from Valdez's Visitor Center at 212 Titikien Street, ☎ (907) 835-2686. Tours depart daily at 10:00 am, 1:00 pm and 7:30 pm and the cost for adults is $15.

Other excellent excursions from Valdez include a rafting trip on the Lowe River through **Keystone Canyon**, one of the most spectacular sites in all of Alaska. Among the many scenic highlights of this trip is 900-foot-high Bridal Veil Falls and the small, but no less beautiful, Horsetail Falls. There are also bus trips that traverse portions of Keystone Canyon and Thompson Pass on their way to the **Worthington Glacier**. This large retreating glacier is 30 miles from Valdez and is one of Alaska's most accessible. These trips allow you to get extremely close to the very base of the glacier.

A final possibility is a flightseeing trip to the Columbia Glacier, stopping on the glacier itself. If you haven't taken a flightseeing trip yet, you should consider it here, especially since the Valdez area generally has much better weather than other ports along the Inside Passage. As a result, your views are less likely to be impeded by mist or clouds, and you'll almost certainly be able to land on the glacier.

Virtually all of the optional tours take a spin through downtown Valdez. Most of them last about two hours so you'll definitely be able to fit in at least one, if not two.

Note that if you're on a cruise that doesn't include Valdez as a port, it is possible to reach it by land from Anchorage. Take the Glenn Highway (Route 1) north to Glenallen and then Alaska 4 (the Richardson Highway) south to Valdez. The total one-way distance is approximately 100 miles. This makes for an excellent side-trip either in one long day or overnight. All of the tours mentioned can be arranged for individual travelers. Contact the Valdez Chamber of Commerce for further information (see *Addenda*, page 199).

Accommodations

Keystone Hotel, 401 Egan Street, ☎ (907) 835-3851. 107 rooms. $. Convenient downtown location within walking distance of the ferry terminal. Decent accommodations. Great breakfast room with fantastic view.

Valdez Village Inn, Richardson Highway & Meals Avenue, ☎ (907) 835-4445. 100 Rooms. $$. One of the nicer places in town, the hotel also has a good restaurant on the premises along with a fitness center with whirlpool and sauna.

Westmark Valdez Hotel, 100 Fidalgo Drive, ☎ (907) 835-4391 or (800) 544-0970. 97 rooms. $$-$$$. Nice location overlooking the small boat harbor. Rooms are attractive and vary quite a bit in size. Ask to see your room first, since there is little or no difference in room rates. Restaurant on premises.

Seward

The town of Seward is set on the scenic Kenai Peninsula, about 125 miles from Anchorage. It is the ending point for cruises that go beyond the Inside Passage to the Gulf of Alaska. As such it is not so much a port of call, but the beginning of the mainland portion of your Alaska journey. Even if you're not going beyond Anchorage, you should take the time to see what Seward has to offer. Like Valdez, there's not that much in the town itself, but it is the gateway to areas of extraordinary beauty as well as a haven for wildlife.

Seward was established in 1902 due to its year-round ice-free waters. It was determined that the site would be a good place for the beginning of the Alaska Railroad, a status that it still holds today. Located on Resurrection Bay, Seward is home to about 3,000 people.

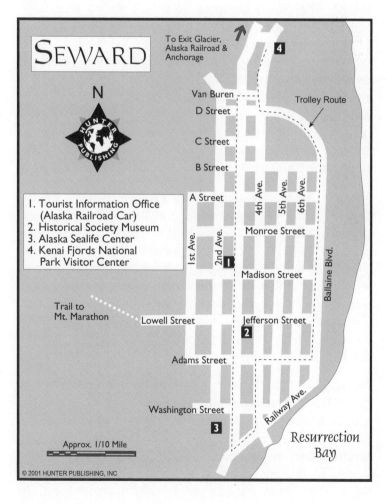

SEWARD

To Exit Glacier, Alaska Railroad & Anchorage

4

N

Van Buren
D Street

Trolley Route

C Street

B Street

4th Ave.
5th Ave.
6th Ave.

A Street

1. Tourist Information Office
   (Alaska Railroad Car)
2. Historical Society Museum
3. Alaska Sealife Center
4. Kenai Fjords National
   Park Visitor Center

Monroe Street

1st Ave.
2nd Ave.

1

Madison Street

Ballaine Blvd.

Trail to
Mt. Marathon

Lowell Street

Jefferson Street

2

Adams Street

Washington Street

3

Railway Ave.

Resurrection
Bay

Approx. 1/10 Mile

© 2001 HUNTER PUBLISHING, INC

Mount Marathon provides a 3,000-foot backdrop to the town. You can climb to the top without too much difficulty. In fact, a yearly marathon race begins and ends at the summit.

You can easily navigate most of the sights within Seward on foot. However, if you want to save some shoe leather or explore some of the points of interest located to the north of downtown, then the Seward Trolley is a convenient way to get around. The trolley operates every day during the Alaska cruise season from 10:00 am until 7:00 pm and costs only $1.50 per ride. An even better buy is the $3 all-day pass. For those taking a walking tour of the small downtown area, you should begin at the Visitor Information Center, which is housed in an old Alaska Railroad car located only a few blocks from the cruise ship terminal. The nearby **Seward & Resurrection Bay Historical Society Museum**, 336 3rd Avenue, ☎ (907) 224-3902, contains exhibits on local history. The adult admission price is $2.

Seward's major attraction is the excellent **Alaska Sealife Center**, at the very beginning (or end, depending on how you look at it) of the Alaska Highway at Milepost 0, ☎ (907) 224-6300 or (800) 224-2525. The large facility has been open only a few years and the 115,000-square-foot marine science center re-creates the natural habitats of many native species, including sea lions and puffins. Many exhibits are dedicated to the preservation of the environment. The adult admission price is $13 but this is one of the more interesting attractions of its kind.

The main sights in the surrounding area are all connected with **Kenai Fjords National Park**. The largest portion of the park is located along the coast south of Seward and is, unfortunately, not visited by cruise ships ending their journey at Seward. However, tours are available, which take one of two forms. The first are boat trips lasting from four to eight hours that explore the majestic coastal mountains and some of the

many inlets in Kenai Fjords. Views of some of the eight glaciers leading off the vast Harding Icefield are common, and
you'll also see a wide variety of marine wildlife that is so abundant in this area. Much of the wildlife is seen on and around
the islands that comprise the **Alaska Maritime National
Wildlife Refuge**. The Chiswell Islands, off the coast of Kenai
Fjords, are teeming with sea lions. It seems as if they're just
waiting for you to come and look at them. Whales are frequently spotted. You can also flightsee over the fjords. While
this method doesn't give you the close-ups of the beautiful
coastline or wildlife, it does take you over the Harding Icefield,
the only way this 700-square-mile ice wilderness can be prop-
erly seen. Either way (or both) makes a wonderful excursion.
Among the many tour operators (should you decide not to
book the tour on your ship) are **Kenai Coastal Tours**,
☎ (800) 770-9119; **Kenai Fjords Tours**, ☎ (800) 478-8068;
Renown Charters & Tours, ☎ (907) 224-3806; and **Scenic
Mountain Air**, ☎ (907) 288-3646. Most boat operators have
several options available that last from about four hours to a
full day and range in price from about $25 to $100.
Flightseeing can range up to about $250 depending upon itin-
erary.

A few miles north of town, **Exit Glacier** can be reached by bus
tour or by car (perfect for those finishing their cruise and pick-
ing up a rental car here). From the parking area it is a nice easy
stroll over paved paths to the very foot of the glacier. Of all the
glaciers you can visit, this one is very likely to be the one you
come closest to. Depending on conditions, the Park Rangers
might allow you within several feet of the glacier's face. Numerous waterfalls on the side of the glacier make it a very picturesque scene. For the more adventurous there's a hiking trail
leading to excellent viewing points above the glacier. Exit Glacier is more than 60,000 years old. Although it may retreat as
much as two feet a day during the summer, it's been advancing since the early 1990s an average of 70 feet per year.

If you can spare 90 minutes, here's something that is fun and exciting – and very Alaskan! **Ididaride Summer Sled Dog Tours**, Old Exit Glacier Road, ☎ (907) 224-8607 or (800) 478-4139, will take you on a two-mile journey through Box Canyon on a wheeled sled pulled by a dog team. You also get to tour the dog kennel, play with the husky puppies and see a training demonstration. The sled ride is captained by an experienced rider from the famed Iditarod Sled Race. (Notice the play on the name – *I-Did-A-Ride*. Get it?) The cost is $28.

Accommodations

Best Western Hotel Seward, 221 Fifth Avenue, ☎ (907) 224-2378 or (800) 528-1234. 38 rooms. $$$$. Convenient in-town location. Nice décor, especially if you get a room facing the bay. Attractive public areas are decorated with Native Alaskan art work.

Edgewater Suites, Seward Small Boat Harbor, ☎ (907) 224-8999. 28 rooms. $$$. This relatively small all-suite facility is decorated with an Alaskan "Cannery Row" theme. The facilities are excellent and many rooms have wonderful views of glaciers and mountains on the other side of the bay.

Seward Windsong Lodge, Exit Glacier Road, ☎ (907) 224-7116 or (888) 959-9590. 72 rooms. $$$. In a secluded mountain setting, the Windsong Lodge offers excellent accommodations in an attractive manner that combines modern and traditional features. There are many nice touches such as the hand-carved furniture. The Lodge is built of native wood and fits in beautifully with the surroundings.

Homer

This small town, once primarily a fishing community, and still dependent on fishing for much of its livelihood, has become a thriving artist colony. Perhaps its pretty setting is the reason. The town sits perched below a long bluff that rises to a height of more than 1,000 feet. An even more prominent feature of Homer is the **Homer Spit**, a very narrow strip of land that juts out from the town for five miles into Kachemak Bay.

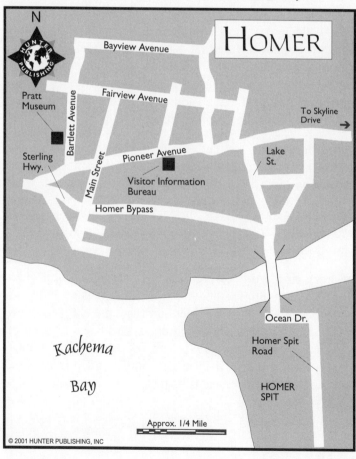

It's likely that only a few readers will be visiting Homer because it is not currently a port of call on any major cruise line itinerary. However, it can be easily reached by ferry or some of the small ship tours.

You can always visit it after the cruise portion of your trip as a side trip from Seward or Anchorage. Visitors should drive out onto the Spit for a good view of the bluffs that overlook the town. Beachcombing along the Spit is a popular diversion for residents and tourists alike. The main attraction within Homer is the **Pratt Museum**, 3779 Bartlett Avenue, just north of Pioneer Avenue, ☎ (907) 235-8635. The museum houses the usual collection of Indian artifacts, although this one emphasizes the Eskimo culture that is barely touched on in Panhandle community museums. The Pratt Museum is best known for its exhibits on marine life, including a number of large aquarium tanks. Summer hours are from 10:00 am until 8:00 pm and the admission is $4.

Several art galleries are scattered throughout town and display the works of the artists who make Homer a home for at least part of the year.

Those looking for a little light reading while in Homer should try the **Book Store,** Eagle Quality Center, 436 Sterling Highway, ☎ (907) 235-7497.

Drive up to **Skyline Drive**, which traverses the top of the bluffs for several miles above town. The top is covered with colorful wildflowers in summer and there are excellent views of the Spit, town, Kachemak Bay and even some of the glaciers that come off of the Harding Icefield. For those that didn't take the flightseeing tour of the icefield from Seward, it can be done from Homer as well. These trips include a stop on the icefield itself, weather permitting.

One of the best tours that can be taken, especially for wildlife enthusiasts, is the **Gull Island Rookery Tour**. A short boat ride from Homer leads you to three small islands where, in summer, more than 15,000 birds nest. One of the islands is shaped like an inverted ice cream cone. In addition to gulls there are cormorants, colorful puffins and many other species. The surface of all of the tiny rocky islands is almost entirely covered with birds. It's unlikely that you'll see a larger concentration of birds anywhere else in your Alaska trip unless you're venturing out to some of the most remote islands much farther to the north. Contact **Homer Ocean Charters**, ☎ (800) 426-6212.

Accommodations

Best Western Bidarka Inn, 575 Sterling Highway, ☎ (907) 235-8148 or (888) 528-1234. 74 rooms. $$. An unpretentious motel with clean and comfortable rooms and a decent restaurant.

Land's End, 4786 Homer Spit Road, ☎ (907) 235-0400. 61 rooms. $$. Nice rooms and the pleasant Chart Room Restaurant is the best in town. Land's End has a great location at the end of the Spit – the views are fantastic.

Pioneer Inn, 244 Pioneer Avenue, ☎ (907) 235-5670. 7 rooms. $. This is a simple little facility but it's quite comfortable and it represents a good value.

Some Other Ports

That about concludes a list of the possible ports that are on the itineraries of the major cruise lines as well as most of the small ship operators. There are a few other ports that we know of that are visited by some small ships, including **Metlakatla**, a tiny community at the beginning of the Inside Passage south of Ketchikan; and **Kodiak**, on an island in the Gulf of Alaska south of the Kenai Peninsula. The former doesn't have any particular points of interest, but the attraction is its authenticity – it's not a tourist town like most places along the Inside Passage. Kodiak is great for the outdoor enthusiast as there are ample opportunities for fishing, wildlife viewing and similar activities. **Petersburg** on the Inside Passage also falls in this category, although it is a little larger than the towns just mentioned. Among other destinations for a few small ships are uninhabited or barely inhabited islands. These are not the kinds of places where you'll get that much out of them wandering about on your own. Those itineraries that include this type of call will have planned activities for you.

Beyond The Cruise

Anchorage

With a population of approximately 260,000, Anchorage is home to 42% of Alaska's population, with considerably more living in towns clustered around the city, especially to the north. Anchorage is not what you'd expect from Alaska – its downtown has a modern skyline and for the most part it looks much like any American city of comparable size. It's the commercial, cultural and recreational capital of the state and has more people working in government than the capital city of Juneau! Although it's spread out, most of the major attractions are within walking distance of one another in the compact downtown area.

There is also good public transportation via the city's bus system, called the "People Mover." The buses reach most visitor attractions of note. They run weekdays from 6 am until 10 pm. Weekend and holiday service is, unfortunately, limited. There's a free downtown ride zone called DASH, which runs along 5th and 6th Avenues between Denali and K Streets. DASH hours are weekdays from 9:00 am until 3:00 pm and 6:00 pm to 8:00 pm as well as all day on weekends. Otherwise, the fare is $1 for adults and 50¢ for children. Transfers are 10¢. A full-day adult pass is an excellent buy at only $2.50. Most routes originate at the People Mover Transit Center at 6th Avenue and G Street. Full information on routes is available at the center, or you can call ☎ (907) 343-6543. However, for traveling to attractions in the outlying areas of town there's no substitute for a car. As with any large city there can be parking and traffic problems, but for the most part, any congestion will seem quite manageable compared to that of most urban areas in the Lower 48.

There's hardly a place in Alaska that isn't in a scenic setting and Anchorage is no exception. At the head of the 220-mile-long Cook Inlet, Anchorage sits where the inlet splits into two "arms" called the Knik and Turnagain. The latter was named by Captain James Cook when he reached the end and found that he could proceed no farther, forcing him to "turn again." The downtown area sits atop a bluff looking out on the Knik Arm and part of the Cook Inlet.

Cruise ship passengers will almost always arrive in Anchorage from Seward either via bus or the Alaska Railroad. From time to time there are some cruise ship operators who decide to use the port of Anchorage but this is definitely the exception to the rule. The Alaska Railroad terminal is walking distance from downtown but, depending upon where you're headed, there is taxi service available. If you're bused in, the drop-off point will vary from one cruise line to another, but it will always be somewhere in downtown (usually at the hotel the cruise line has picked for any optional stay in Anchorage).

Anchorage, especially downtown, is a very easy city when it comes to finding your way around. Downtown is a neat grid pattern. Numbered avenues run east to west and lettered streets run from north to south. At the intersection of 4th Avenue and F Street is Anchorage's **Log Cabin Visitor Center**. Here's where you can collect information on everything that is happening within the city and beyond and seek further assistance about places to see, hotel accommodations and so forth. The cabin itself is an odd but pretty sight, sitting as it does in the middle of a modern city. In summer it's bedecked with hanging baskets of flowers and the surrounding grounds are picturesque. Anchorage calls itself the "Crossroads of the World" and outside the cabin is a wooden signpost showing the direction and air mileage to places all around the world.

On the side of the building directly across F Street from the Visitor Center is a mural of Alaskan scenes. We've already mentioned that murals are common in Alaska, and nowhere will you find more in quantity, variety and size than in Anchorage. In case you're interested in seeing even more of this local means of artistic expression, some of the better ones are close by. These include one in the State Historical Museum at 4th and F Street (160 feet long), another depicting the route of the Iditarod Dog Sled Race at 4th and D Street and murals in the form of wool tapestries showing scenes of Alaskan history in the National Bank of Alaska Building at 4th and E Street.

The centrally located Visitor Center is an excellent place to begin a walking tour of downtown Anchorage. At the same intersection, but located diagonally across from the Log Cabin, is the **Alaska Public Lands Information Center**, 605 W. 4th Avenue, ☎ (907) 271-2737. In the former Federal Building, the center has exhibits about the geology and wildlife on lands owned by the federal and state governments, which represents a sizable portion of the state, including almost all of the most scenic areas. During the summer the Center is open daily from 8:00 am until 8:00 pm and there is no admission charge. From here proceed north on E Street until 3rd, turn right and walk one block. This is the **Earthquake Buttress Area**. The 1964 Easter earthquake brought terrible destruction to Anchorage. At this point a large chunk of the bluff gave way, dropping more than 20 feet. It has been filled with gravel to stabilize the area. At 2nd and E is the **Alaska State Monu-**

ment, which includes a bust of Dwight Eisenhower, President of the United States at the time of Alaska's admission to the Union. Here, too, is the **Ship Creek Viewpoint** where you can see the busy freighter traffic bringing goods to and from Anchorage. Beneath the bluff is the **Alaska Railroad Depot**. If you're heading to the interior of Alaska via the Alaska Railroad you don't have to make a special trip to see it now, but if you're going to be journeying by car or not going beyond Anchorage then you might want to take a detour in order to explore its very ornate interior.

Take 2nd Avenue to its junction with 1st Avenue and then turn left back toward the depot. Proceed west on 3rd Avenue until H Street and you'll have a fine view of the **Port of Anchorage** again lying beneath the high bluff.

Anchorage contains a number of unique sculptures. The first of these is the **Last Blue Whale Statue** on L Street between 3rd and 4th. This somewhat abstract work is sculpted in fiberglass and rises above the second story of the building behind it. At the end of 3rd Avenue is **Resolution Park** that contains the **Captain Cook Monument**. The park is a pleasant place to view the Cook Inlet and mountains beyond, as well as a good spot to take a rest from your walking tour amid benches and flowers.

Head right for one block on 5th Avenue until you reach M Street. Turn right again at this junction. The **Oscar Anderson House Museum**, 420 M Street, ☎ (907) 274-2336 was built in 1915 and was home to one of Anchorage's early residents and businessman. The Anderson family figured prominently in the commercial development of the city. The house has been refurbished and is furnished in period style. A number of other historic homes are located in this part of town. Information is available at the Anderson House. Open Tuesday through Saturday from 11:00 am until 4:00 pm. The admission is $3 for adults.

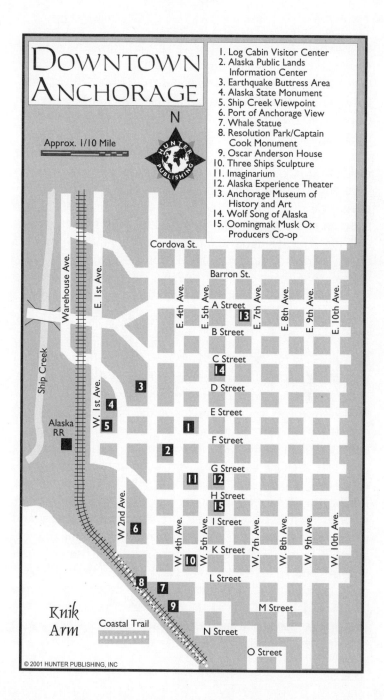

Downtown Anchorage

N

Approx. 1/10 Mile

1. Log Cabin Visitor Center
2. Alaska Public Lands Information Center
3. Earthquake Buttress Area
4. Alaska State Monument
5. Ship Creek Viewpoint
6. Port of Anchorage View
7. Whale Statue
8. Resolution Park/Captain Cook Monument
9. Oscar Anderson House
10. Three Ships Sculpture
11. Imaginarium
12. Alaska Experience Theater
13. Anchorage Museum of History and Art
14. Wolf Song of Alaska
15. Oomingmak Musk Ox Producers Co-op

HUNTER PUBLISHING

Ship Creek

Alaska RR

Knik Arm

Coastal Trail

Warehouse Ave.
E. 1st Ave.
W. 1st Ave.
W. 2nd Ave.
E. 4th Ave.
E. 5th Ave.
E. 7th Ave.
E. 8th Ave.
E. 9th Ave.
E. 10th Ave.
W. 4th Ave.
W. 5th Ave.
W. 7th Ave.
W. 8th Ave.
W. 9th Ave.
W. 10th Ave.

Cordova St.
Barron St.
A Street
B Street
C Street
D Street
E Street
F Street
G Street
H Street
I Street
K Street
L Street
M Street
N Street
O Street

© 2001 HUNTER PUBLISHING, INC

This is the farthest point in the walking tour from the center of downtown, and now it's time to head back toward the center. On K Street between 4th and 5th is the **Three Ships Sculpture**, which depicts the voyage of discovery led by Captain Cook. At 737 W. 5th Avenue at the intersection of G Street is the **Imaginarium**, ☎ (907) 276-3179, a hands-on science discovery center that is interesting for all ages, but especially for children. It is open daily from 10:00 am to 6:00 pm (noon to 5:00 pm on Sunday) and the admission is $6 for adults. Located nearby at 604 H Street is the **Oomingmak Musk Ox Producers Co-op**, ☎ (907) 272-9225. This free attraction will allow you to become familiar with the fine fabric called qiviut, made from arctic musk ox wool, which is eight times warmer than sheep's wool although it is the same weight. The scarves and other qiviut items are made by Alaskan natives and can be purchased at the co-op for a good price.

At the corner of 6th and C Street is the fascinating **Wolf Song of Alaska**, ☎ (907) 274-9653. The large free exhibit will bring you into a face-to-face encounter with wild Alaskan wolves. Although the museum traces many myths and legends associated with wolves, the emphasis is on the history of the animal and its surprising relationship with humans. Interesting and educational for adults and children. The museum is open daily and there is an admission charge. Call for further information. A few blocks away at 6th and F in the **Alaska Center for the Performing Arts**, two IMAX films are shown daily during the summer months. The films feature the natural scenery and wildlife of the state and, although changed from time to time, are always technically excellent and visually stunning. Call ☎ (907) 263-ARTS for schedules and ticket information. Another possibility for IMAX lovers is the **Alaska Experience Theater**, 6th and G, ☎ (907) 276-3730. The films here are similar to those at the arts center. The Alaska Experience also has an interesting exhibit on the great Alaskan earthquake of 1964.

The **Anchorage Museum of History and Art**, 121 W. 7th Avenue, ☎ (907) 343-4326, is a large museum covering many aspects of Alaskan history and the native cultures of the state. Large dioramas in the Alaska Gallery are of special interest. The museum is open daily from 9:00 am until 9:00 pm (until 6:00 pm on Saturday evening) and the adult admission price is $5.

The walking tour as described here will take around three hours to complete on a cursory basis, but could require several additional hours if you spend a lot of time in the various museums along the route and you decide to view an IMAX film or two. If you have a very limited amount of time you might want to consider a guided city tour. There is a one-hour tour via **Anchorage Trolley Tours**, ☎ (907) 276-5603 and a three-hour trip offered by **Gray Line of Alaska**, ☎ (800) 478-6388. The cost for the shorter tour is $10, while the longer trip is $40. Reservations are suggested.

There are several good attractions that are still located within or close to the city of Anchorage but outside of the downtown core. These require using a bus, taxi or rental car for transportation. **Elmendorf Air Force Base** to the north (tours given usually once a week during the summer, ☎ (907) 552-5755 for information) is interesting to military hardware buffs, while nature lovers will be more attracted to the **Eagle River Nature Center** in Chugach State Park. This is reached by Eagle River Road east from the Glenn Highway. It has hiking and wildlife. Nearby, also off the Glenn Highway is an easy one-mile walk through a deep canyon to **Thunderbird Falls**. Heading in the opposite direction from downtown is the **Alaska Zoo**, ☎ (907) 346-3242. To get there, take the Alaska Highway south from downtown for about eight miles, then turn east on O'Malley Road. The zoo's 30 acres specialize in native animals. The cost of admission is $6. **Earthquake Park** is west from downtown at the end of Northern Lights Boulevard. The park provides good views of the Cook Inlet and downtown, backed by the beautiful Chugach Mountains. For those of you who love to walk, the Coastal Trail runs through the park and extends all the way to downtown.

The **Alaska Aviation Heritage Museum**, 4721 Aircraft Drive, ☎ (907) 248-5325, is located near the airport on the south shore of Lake Hood. It has more than 20 vintage aircraft. Most of the planes were in service in Alaska during the 1930s and are quite rare. Visitors can see restoration work in progress. The museum is open daily from 9:00 am to 6:00 pm and costs $6.

One final attraction definitely worth seeing while in town is the **Alaska Native Heritage Center**, 8800 Heritage Center Drive, ☎ (800) 315-6608. To get there, go about three miles east of downtown via the Glenn Highway to the Muldoon Road exit, then head north to Heritage Drive. The Center covers almost 30 acres and does an excellent job of informing visitors about all of Alaska's various native cultures. Authentic tribal homes represent five different native "villages" built around a pond, and tribe members conduct daily activities. There is also a program of entertainment. Visitors are encouraged to participate. The center is open daily from 9:00 am until 9:00 pm. The admission is on the steep side at $20 for adults ($15 for children over age six) but you could spend several interesting hours here.

As Alaska's largest city, Anchorage is also the place where you'll find the greatest variety of shopping and cultural activities. Downtown contains a number of large modern shopping malls and there are even more scattered throughout the city. However, if you came to Alaska to shop, chances are you'll be looking for native handicrafts. All genuine Native American-made articles have a label to that effect, so be sure to look for it before purchasing, especially if you're buying in a tourist souvenir shop. Among the best places in Anchorage to buy

Native crafts are at the **Taheta Art and Culture Co-op**, 5th and A; and the previously mentioned **Oomingmak Musk Ox Producers Co-op**. The former has a wide variety of handicrafts and makes an interesting place to visit, while the latter specializes in warm, incredibly soft scarves and other garments produced from Arctic musk-ox wool. Although fur garments are a controversial item these days there are still many people who want such items. If you are interested, then head for the **Alaska Fur Exchange**, Old Seward Highway and Tudor Road. They also have a large selection of Native-made arts and crafts. A wide selection of authentic carvings, jewelry and other items is available at **Alaska Unique**, 3601 Minnesota Drive. If you're looking for a gift package of Alaskan seafood to send to someone back home, check out **10th & M Seafoods**. Their main store is at 1020 M Street and they also have a branch at 301 Muldoon Road.

Cultural entertainment in the form of symphony, professional theater, dance and even opera are all available in Anchorage, concentrated mostly in the **Alaska Center for the Performing Arts** bounded by 5th, 6th, F and G Streets. The large, modern complex sits in an attractively landscaped park. Inquire at the box office about events and tickets, or check with the Log Cabin Visitor Center to find out what's available at the Performing Arts Center and throughout the city.

Around Anchorage

One of the nicest things about visiting Anchorage is that it is surrounded by magnificent scenery and almost unlimited recreational opportunities. Now that we've explored Anchorage itself, it's time to focus our attention to the sights and activities of nearby areas that can be turned into a great full-day excursion from Anchorage. You might find yourself needing an additional day if you decide to take some of the many available

Beyond the Cruise

boat rides that will be described later. There are several attractions located to the north of Anchorage in an area known as the Matanuska Valley. However, since it is likely that most visitors will be heading north to Denali and possibly Fairbanks, this area will be discussed later (see section on Matanuska Valley following the Fairbanks section, page 178). You would be best off touring this area either on the way to or from Denali and the interior.

When it comes to natural beauty near Anchorage, one thing is definitely true – the majority of the best sights are located to the south of the city in the northern portion of the Kenai Peninsula or to the southeast in the Chugach Mountains (and National Forest of the same name). Within the latter area is Portage Glacier and the extreme northwest corner of Prince William Sound. The Seward Highway (referred to south of Anchorage as Alaska Highway 1) has been designated as a National Scenic Byway because of the remarkable panorama it affords from end to end. The initial part of the route from Anchorage parallels the Alaska Railroad along the Turnagain Arm and is the initial means of access to all of the areas described in this section. The excellent road is sometimes down at the water level but frequently climbs the lower slopes of the mountains which hug the coast. A number of attractions are within a short distance of the road, but the Seward Highway itself is a primary attraction, containing more than 30 pull-outs from which to admire the scenery. Many trailheads begin at these pull-outs and lead up into the mountains for even more dramatic views. Unfortunately, most of these are steep and strenuous. Details on trails can be obtained from the Supervisor of the Chugach State Park.

Just a few miles south of Anchorage is the first major point of interest, the **Anchorage Coastal Wildlife Refuge**, more commonly known as the Potter Marsh Waterfowl Refuge. It's right off the highway on a broad coastal marsh set in front of picturesque mountains. A long boardwalk traverses the entire area, giving visitors an opportunity to view birds of almost a hundred different species as well as salmon and other fish in the shallow waterways of the marsh.

Soon after the refuge one of the most scenic sections of the Seward Highway begins, where the pull-outs come upon you one after another. Among the best of these is **Beluga Point**, where white beluga whales are commonly spotted during the summer months. Tidal bores often occur here as well (consult Anchorage newspapers for tide times). **Windy Point** and **Falls Creek** also provide great views of mountain and sea, but are best known as places where you're likely to see Dall sheep clinging to the lower slopes. If you stop to get a closer look be very careful not to approach these horned animals – they're wild and might be frightened into charging you in self-defense.

A little beyond the small town of Girdwood is a short cutoff road leading to the year-round **Alyeska Ski Area**. During the summer you can take the chairlift to the summit for an unforgettable view of the Turnagain Arm surrounded by lofty peaks. There are other activities at Alyeska, including carriage rides and hiking trails. Several restaurants are also located here. Back on the main highway will be another well-placed pullout, this one for the **Explorer Glacier Viewpoint**.

Continuing along Seward Highway you'll soon reach another side road, this one extending for five miles to what has become Alaska's most heavily visited attraction – **Portage Glacier Recreation Area**. Here's an outstanding scenic attraction that quickly fills a few hours of your time. The highlight is Portage Glacier itself, a five-mile-long and mile-wide ice floe that is so close it is referred to as a "drive-in" glacier. It sits on Portage Lake and can be viewed from along a lakeside walkway or by taking a boat ride on the MV *Ptarmigan*.

Not to be missed is the **Begich-Boggs Visitor Center**, an outstanding facility that describes in detail the history of Por-

Beyond the Cruise

tage Glacier and the surrounding area. A walk-through model of a glacier is inside the modern building and there is an observation area from which you can view the glacier. This is especially handy should you be here during inclement weather. Other parts of the recreation area have lovely waterfalls cascading down the sheer mountain slopes and there are several hiking trails of varying lengths and difficulty. One of the easier trails is the one-mile route to the base of Byron Glacier, a hanging-type glacier as opposed to Portage, which is a tidewater glacier.

In case you don't have a rental car there are many tours from Anchorage that travel along the Seward Highway and visit Portage Glacier. Once you get to the visitor center by whatever method is most convenient for you, you can take an hourlong boat ride that departs from near the visitor center five times daily and costs $25 for adults. Complete packages from Anchorage, including the cruise, are also available. Contact **Portage Glacier Cruises**, ☎ (907) 277-5581.

Continuing south from Portage, which lies at the junction with the Seward Highway, it's 42 miles to an important junction on the Kenai Peninsula. At that point Highway 1 heads southwest and leads to Homer, some 130 miles distant, while the Seward Highway continues south as Highway 9 for 37 more miles to Seward. Both routes offer the beautiful mountain and coastal scenery of the Kenai Peninsula and are well maintained from the beginning to end.

The sights of the Seward area (including Kenai Fjords National Park) and Homer were previously described in the *Ports of Call* chapter for those who visit these communities by cruise ship or other means. Anyone making the overland journey to them from Anchorage should refer to that chapter now for details on what to see. If you are traveling beyond the Portage Glacier area from Anchorage it makes sense to make this an overnight excursion.

Here are some other tour boat operators that are worthwhile looking into depending upon your time availability and how well your cruise covered the waters of the Prince William Sound and the Kenai Peninsula. **Glacier Quest**, ☎ (888) 305-2515, offers trips to both the Kenai Fjords (for $99) and to the Prince William Sound ($115). Both include lunch in the price. The **Klondike Express** departs from Whittier and has a $119 Prince William Sound cruise. ☎ (800) 544-0529 or ☎ (907) 276-8023 in Anchorage. **Renown Charters & Tours** has a variety of itineraries in the Kenai Peninsula and also offers transportation from Anchorage. The price ranges from $49 to $139 depending upon the length of the trip and whether or not you need transportation to the embarkation point. Call ☎ (800) 655-3806 or ☎ (907) 272-1961 in Anchorage. See the listing in the *Addenda* for the phone numbers of several other companies offering a wide range of day trips including **Kenai Fjords Tours** and **Major Marine Tours**.

If you get the urge to read more about Alaska upon your arrival in Anchorage then the following stores will have plenty of detailed books on Anchorage and Alaska as a whole, in addition to light reading material. **Cook Inlet Book Company**, 415 W. 5th Ave., ☎ (907) 258-4544; **Cyrano's Books**, 413 D Street, ☎ (907) 274-5299.

Accommodations

Anchorage Hilton, 500 W. 3rd Avenue, ☎ (907) 245-0322 or (800) 445-8667. 591 rooms. $$$$. A big and modern city center hotel with lots of dining and shopping options and all the luxury and facilities you expect from Hilton.

Comfort Inn Ship Creek, 111 W. Ship Creek Avenue, ☎ (907) 277-6887 or (800) 363-6887. 100 rooms. $$$-$$$$.

Nice rooms and public areas not far from downtown attractions and well situated for those who'll be hopping on the Alaska Railroad to points north.

Holiday Inn Downtown, 239 W. 5th Avenue, ☎ (907) 279-8671 or (800) HOLIDAY. 251 rooms. $$$. Excellent location. Attractive public areas and comfortable rooms are the highlights of this spacious property.

Hotel Captain Cook, 939 W. 5th Avenue, ☎ (907) 376-6000 or (800) 843-1950. 565 rooms. $$$$. Perhaps Anchorage's most famous hotel and still, after many years, one of the best. First-class in-room amenities and sophisticated atmosphere in public areas. Many suites in addition to regular rooms. Four excellent restaurants, athletic clubs and shopping arcade.

Longhouse Alaskan Hotel, 4335 Wisconsin Street, ☎ (907) 243-2133. 54 rooms. $$$. Interesting architecture features long log-sided structures with a rustic look. Room interiors are modern and attractively decorated. Pretty lakeside location. Room rate includes continental breakfast.

Merrill Field Inn, 420 Sitka Street, ☎ (907) 276-4547 or (800) 898-4547. 39 rooms. $$. You have to go away from downtown to get reasonable prices in Anchorage, but this attractive little motel is only about a mile from the heart of the action. Some units have efficiency kitchens.

Regal Alaskan Hotel, 4800 Spenard Road, ☎ (907) 243-2300 or (800) 544-0553. 248 rooms. $$$$. This luxurious facility has a wide variety of tastefully appointed rooms and suites. The lobby is filled with hunting trophies and photographs depicting local history. Fine restaurant.

Sheraton Anchorage, 401 E. 6th Avenue, ☎ (907) 276-8700 or (800) 325-3535. 375 rooms. $$$$. A modern high-rise hotel that's typical of what you would expect from a city-center Sheraton. Good restaurants.

Westmark Anchorage, 720 W. 5th Avenue, ☎ (907) 276-7676 or (800) 544-0970. 198 rooms. $$$-$$$$. With an excellent downtown location, oversized rooms and beautiful décor, the Westmark is one of Anchorage's premier lodging establishments.

Voyager Hotel, 501 K Street, ☎ (907) 277-9501 or (800) 247-9070. 38 rooms. $$$. This is one of the few good downtown hotels in this price category. The rooms are oversized and nicely decorated in a European style. The on-premises Corsair Restaurant is one of the better eateries in town. Room rate includes continental breakfast.

The Interior

This chapter will be broken down into several sections. These are *Heading North,* which covers the area between Anchorage and Denali; *Denali National Park*; *Fairbanks*; and the *Matanuska Valley.* All of these areas are common add-ons to Alaska cruise vacations.

Before getting started on the first area, however, we must address the two main methods for seeing the interior of Alaska. These are, of course, by guided tour and on your own. Guided tours can be arranged as a continuation of your cruise or separately. While booking through your cruise line may not be as cheap as arranging interior tours on your own, it does provide continuity between the two portions of your trip. Most guided tours use a combination of motor coach and the Alaska Railroad. If this part of your vacation is arranged by the cruise lines, you get to stay in the domed cars on the train, which offer a better view of the scenery.

If you're going to be driving, car rentals are available throughout Alaska and are especially easy to find in Anchorage. The distance from Anchorage to Denali National Park is 240 miles and another 125 miles if you continue to Fairbanks. All of this is via Alaska Highway 3, a well-paved road that won't present any driving problems and is better known as the George Parks Highway. Distances to sights south from Anchorage are much less and shouldn't discourage anyone. Individual travelers going to Denali and/or Fairbanks can also book passage on the Alaska Railroad.

Heading North

The area between Anchorage and Denali National Park is sparsely populated. But there are a few towns and you're never that far from civilization, so finding a place to have lunch or fill the car up with gas is never a problem. Although some of the larger towns may have a motel or two, standards are generally below those found in other parts of the country. As the drive to Denali takes less than a day, you should plan on staying overnight in or near the park itself. For the most part it's a very pleasant and scenic ride.

Among the towns you'll be passing through or near to are **Wasilla, Willow,** and **Talkeetna.** Wasilla and Talkeetna each have a museum focusing on the local history and a collection of native artifacts. Wasilla's **Museum of Alaska Transportation & Industry**, Milepost 47, ☎ (907) 376-1211, is one of the more interesting possible stops en route. The adult admission is $5. Within the vicinity of Wasilla (and the other towns along the route) there are often state parks or wilderness areas with opportunities for hiking. Most trails are primitive or difficult and are generally a few miles off the main road. Many travelers who are simply extending their cruise will not have the time for this type of exploration. If you do, the towns all have visitor information centers that will be glad to give you advice and directions on these out-of-the-way places.

A few miles north of Wasilla is the town of Willow. While there isn't anything of great appeal in town, you might be interested in knowing that Willow gained some notoriety back in the 1970s when it was selected to be the site of a new state capital to replace Juneau. Many people, both then and now, felt that the capital should be more centrally located and closer to the population center of Anchorage. The issue resurfaces from time to time, but it doesn't look as if Willow is ever going to become home to the statehouse.

Talkeetna is 14 miles off Parks Highway via a good side road beginning at Milepost 98.7. A mining community established just after the turn of the century, Talkeetna maintains the same atmosphere today – mainly dirt roads through a town of 400 log cabins. **Talkeetna Historical Society Museum** is housed in four old buildings, including a school. In addition to the mildly interesting exhibits here, this is the place to pick up a map, which will direct you on a walking tour past the town's historic structures, many of which have been restored. Leaving Talkeetna, you have to return to Highway 3 the same way you came in.

Once you pass by Milepost 100 or so the scenery becomes even more impressive and the Parks Highway has a number of pull-outs, so do take advantage of them. **Denali State Park** is a largely undeveloped wilderness area to the south of Denali National Park. The very best scenery of the entire route is on this portion of the highway. From Denali State Park you'll have an excellent distant view of Mt. McKinley (weather permitting) and many other peaks, as well as the glaciers on the mountain's southern slope. The Glacier Overlook at Milepost 135.2 is an especially good place to stop for a stretch and take in the scenery. The interior of the park has many trails, but they're rather difficult.

Denali National Park

Denali is one of America's largest national parks, covering a mind-boggling six million acres. It was established in 1917 as McKinley National Park. Its single most prominent feature is Mt. McKinley, one of the world's tallest peaks at 20,320 feet. In some ways it is the highest peak because the surrounding terrain is generally not at a great altitude. McKinley stands approximately 18,000 feet higher than the surrounding landscape. Denali today is known as much for its diverse wildlife as for the "High One," which is the native term for the mountain. The most common of the larger animals found here are the almost 3,000 caribou, 2,500 Dall sheep, 2,000 moose, 200 wolves and about 500 grizzly and black bears. There are dozens of other species within the park, but the ones mentioned are the result of a survey of park visitors and were spotted by more than 80% of respondents. Denali also covers a number of different environmental zones, including *taiga* (far northern forests of coniferous trees) and *tundra* (nearly flat and treeless plains).

For those making the journey from Anchorage by train, the Alaska Railroad has a station right in the park within walking distance of lodging, restaurants and the Visitor Access Center. Although most of the park is inaccessible to those who are not hiking into the back country, there is a single road that extends for 97 miles into the park; however, only the first 14 miles to the Savage River are open to general traffic. Beyond that point the only access is either by shuttle bus or tour bus. (This is because the unpaved road could not handle greater levels of traffic and, even if it could, officials do not want to spoil the pristine environment.) We'll take a look at the shuttle bus method of exploring Denali first. These buses aren't luxury touring vehicles – in fact, some are little more than old-fashioned school buses and aren't very comfortable for a long, bumpy ride. Nor are they tour buses – that is, no narration is provided – but there is a charge of between $7 and $27, depending on how far you're going. There are also passes good for unlimited use on the buses for either three or six days. Drivers will gladly stop when wildlife is seen so pictures can be taken and also at especially scenic points. Stops are made at approximately 1½-hour intervals, where there are restroom facilities. (Once you get on the bus there are virtually no facilities in the park, so bring food, warm clothing and insect repellent along with you.) Do get off the bus from time to time to explore. Rangers at the Visitor Access Center will suggest certain areas based on your interests and physical capabilities. Buses will stop to let you off and you can re-board any bus that comes along once you're on the shuttle route. Getting on a bus in the first place is a problem if you don't have advance reservations, so be sure to book your spot on the bus in advance if at all possible. About half of the seats on each bus are available in advance. ☎ (907) 272-7272 or (800) 622-7275. All other seats are given on a first-come, first-served basis *in person only* up to two days before departure. Sign up at the Visitor Access Center just off Highway 3 the moment you arrive in Denali. Buses leave approximately at half-hour intervals beginning at 6 am. However, the demand is greater than the supply of buses. During the summer you'll usually find no seats available for the day you arrive. For those arriving with fixed hotel reservations and a limited amount of time it probably means not being able to stay around long enough to get on a bus. If you plan on spending several days in the area then it isn't a big deal; you could do other things in Denali for a day or visit Fairbanks and be back in Denali in time for your scheduled departure.

Guided tours on comfortable buses (with lunch provided) are offered twice daily at 6 am and 3 pm. These tours last between six and seven hours depending upon the weather. They don't go as far into the park as the shuttles, but they will allow you to visit the highlights in greater comfort. Advance reservations are strongly suggested since these tours also fill up very quickly, often with cruise passengers on escorted tours. There are also shorter (three-hour) tours which cost about $35 per adult, including a snack. The longer tour provides a full lunch and costs $64. Information and reservations for these trips can be arranged through **Tundra Wildlife Tours**, ☎ (907) 276-7234 or (800) 268-2215. All tours depart from the Denali Park Hotel.

Mt. McKinley first becomes visible from the park road at Milepost 9.4. The capricious weather in Denali often obscures part or all of the mountain for long periods of time. In fact, there is no guarantee that you'll see Mt. McKinley at all during your visit. If you're lucky enough to get a clear day, then the view of the distant perennially white peak is a sight that, alone, is worth the trip from Anchorage. Even better views are afforded from various points farther along the road, all in the area beyond where private vehicles are allowed.

The Riley Creek area is near the park entrance and is the hub for all activities and services. Here you'll find several lodging facilities and restaurants (advance reservations for rooms are an absolute must). A number of trails leave from the Visitor Access Center area. These include Horseshoe Lake Trail (.75 of a mile), Morino Loop Trail (1.5 miles) and Rock Creek Trail (2.3 miles). All are relatively easy. Horseshoe Lake Trail leads to a bluff overlooking a picturesque lake and the Nenana River. Rock Creek Trail leads to the Dog Kennels, which we'll discuss in a few moments. There are several other trails in the area, all of which are more difficult than the ones just mentioned.

Denali is a wilderness area and is very isolated, especially during the winter. Supplies to remote portions of the park and more than an occasional rescue mission must be done by dog-sled, just as in the *Sgt. Preston* TV shows of days gone by! The park maintains its own dog teams, which are housed in kennels a couple of miles from the Visitor Access Center. Sled dog demonstrations are held at 10 am, 2 pm and 4 pm. Private vehicles can park near the kennels or you can walk or take a free bus from the Access Center. It leaves every 30 minutes. Rangers will tell you about the dogs, show you how they're hitched up and take them for a spin around the complex. It's a most interesting and rewarding experience for all. You can visit the dogs at any time throughout the day.

At Milepost 238 of Highway 3, a few miles north of the Denali Park entrance, is the starting point for trips on the Nenana River. These include both scenic float trips and whitewater excursions through a narrow canyon. It's a popular activity. Trips range from two hours to a full day, depending upon the type of adventure. Operators include **Denali Raft Adventures**, ☎ (888) 683-2234. It's a worthwhile diversion and a fulfilling way to spend your time if you are waiting for a shuttle bus.

Accommodations

Denali Bluffs Hotel, George Parks Highway (AK 3), one mile north of park entrance, ☎ (907) 683-7000 or (800) 488-7002. 112 rooms. $$$. One of the newer facilities in the area of Denali, the Bluffs features well-appointed rooms and fabulous views. They have a tour desk in the lobby.

Denali Parks Resorts, off AK 3, inside Denali National Park. ☎ (907) 276-7234 or (800) 276-7234. 534 rooms. $$. A group of accommodations (often known as Denali Park Hotel, one of the constituent properties), these decent rooms are the most convenient for in-park tours and activities. All can be arranged through the hotel front desk. There's a good choice of restaurants.

Beyond the Cruise

Denali Princess Lodge, George Parks Highway (AK 3), 1½ miles north of the park entrance. ☎ (907) 683-2282 or (800) 426-0500. 353 rooms. $$$. Recently expanded and remodeled, what was already the Denali area's most luxurious (and expensive) property is even more so. Unfortunately, if you wind up with one of the smaller rooms, it doesn't meet up to the level of luxury in the public areas. Excellent restaurant.

Denali River Cabins, George Parks Highway (AK 3), immediately south of park entrance. ☎ (907) 683-2500. 104 rooms. $$. Simple but clean and comfortable accommodations either in one of 50 log cabins or in the newer motel section. We like the former because they fit right in with the Denali experience.

Denali Riverview Inn, George Parks Highway (AK 3), one mile north of the park entrance. ☎ (907) 683-2663. 12 rooms. $$. Set in the trees overlooking the Nenana River, this delightful little place has few services but lots of peace and quiet.

Denali Windsor Lodge, George Parks Highway (AK 3), one mile north of the park entrance. ☎ (907) 683-1240 or (800) 208-0200. 48 rooms. $$. Small but very attractive property that combines the look and feel of the wilderness with modern conveniences.

Fairbanks

With a population of about 84,000, Fairbanks is the second-largest city in Alaska. Despite its growth, it retains a strong frontier-style atmosphere. In fact, the streets of downtown are still lined with a large number of log structures. In most ways, Fairbanks is more Alaskan than Anchorage and that alone makes it worthwhile to venture this far north. Fairbanks and its residents proudly reflect their mining community origins.

Downtown – if you can call it that – consists of a few blocks on either side of the main thoroughfare (Cushman Street) stretching from 1st through 12th Avenues. Most of the city is rather spread out and occupies a peninsula formed by the Chena River and the wider island-dotted Tanana River. Additional areas to the north of the Chena are also within Fairbanks proper. The adjacent communities of Ester, Fox and North Pole all comprise greater Fairbanks.

Fairbanks' road connection to Anchorage and other parts south is via the George Parks Highway (the aforementioned State Highway 3). Many visitors avoid the long drive from Anchorage by taking the scenic Alaska Railroad. The train depot is on the north side of the Chena just a few blocks from the Cushman Street bridge and is walking distance to downtown. Near the south side of the bridge are two good places to begin your visit. The first is the **Visitor Information Log Cabin** at 550 1st Avenue and the second is the **Alaska Public Lands Information Center**, 250 Cushman Street. The latter is similar to the one in Anchorage, although smaller. In addition to gathering information, you can view displays about Alaskan wildlife. Other than these two places and the general interest of exploring the quaint downtown, you'll have to venture away from the city center to take in Fairbanks' sights.

The **University of Alaska** campus is home to a fine museum at 907 Yukon Drive. The museum houses a large and interesting collection of items related to Alaska's natural and cultural history, including the gold rush. Two excellent film presentations are shown throughout the day. The first explains the phenomenon of the **aurora borealis,** more commonly known as the Northern Lights, while the other tells about the Northern Inuit culture. The museum admission is $5 but there are additional charges for each of the films. You can also take a guided walking tour of the campus. The tours, which depart from the museum, visit the Geophysical Institute, the agricultural and experimental farm and animal research station.

A couple of short excursions from Fairbanks are worthwhile ways to spend time. The **Riverboat *Discovery*** departs from 1975 Discovery Drive, off Airport Way, at 8:45 am and 2 pm for a 3½-hour journey on the Chena and Tanana Rivers. Wildlife can often be seen and a stop is made at the Athabascan Indian village. Informative guides provide interesting narrative throughout the trip. The adult fare is $40 and reservations are required, so call ☎ (907) 479-6673. North of Fairbanks via the Old Steese Highway (on Highway 6) is *Gold Dredge #8*, ☎ (907) 457-6058. The five-deck ship towers more than 250 feet high and dates from 1928. Interesting 90-minute tours are offered and afterwards you can pan for gold to your heart's content. While this is an interesting stop we think it's overpriced at $20 for adults. It is open daily from 9:00 am to 6:00 pm. About 14 miles north of Fairbanks via the Steese Highway is the **National Oceanic & Atmospheric Administration Satellite Tracking Station** (no phone). Science enthusiasts will enjoy the guided tour of this facility which plays a major role in the United States space program. The free tours depart on the hour weekdays from 8:00 am until 4:00 pm and on Saturday from 9:00 am to 3:00 pm. And while you're on the Steese Highway watch for the turnoff onto Goldstream Road. The latter will take you to a spot overlooking a section of the **Alaska Pipeline**. You may find that viewing a small section of the pipeline doesn't allow for the proper appreciation of the massive scope of the pipeline project. However, you'll still probably agree that the small detour was worth it, especially if your cruise didn't get to Valdez and you weren't able to see the pipeline terminal.

Heading in another direction from Fairbanks is the neighboring town of Ester is the **Ester Gold Camp**, 3660 Main Street, ☎ (907) 479-2500. From Fairbanks take the Parks Highway five miles west to Ester. The camp is the site of a 1904 gold mining community of the Fairbanks Exploration Company. It operated until as recently as 1958. Two shows at the camp relate the "Photosymphony on the Northern Lights" and the "Service with a Smile," a musical revue about the gold rush era. The camp has a restaurant and gift shops as well. Admission to the gold camp is free, but there is a charge of $6 for the Photosymphony and $12 for Service with a Smile. The shows are in the evening and reservations are suggested.

Bookstores in Fairbanks include: **Baker & Baker Booksellers**, University Center Mall, 3627 Airport Rd., #1, ☎ (907) 456-2278; and **Gullivers Used Books**, 3525 College Road, ☎ (907) 474-9574.

Accommodations

Bridgewater Hotel, 723 1st Avenue, ☎ (907) 452-6661 or (800) 528-4916. 94 rooms. $$. Central location. Free transportation to airport and Alaska Railroad depot. Nice rooms; on-site restaurant.

Fairbanks Exploration Inn, 505 Illinois Street, ☎ (907) 451-1920 or (888) 452-1920. 16 rooms. $$$. Large and attractive B&B-style facility that provides a comfortable stay. Some units have kitchen facilities. Friendly and gracious staff.

Fairbanks Princess Riverside Lodge, 4477 Pikes Landing Road, ☎ (907) 455-4477 or (800) 426-0500. 325 rooms. $$$$. Formerly the Fairbanks Princess Hotel, the newly expanded (by 125 rooms) is the biggest and most luxurious property in town, as well as the most expensive. The new décor reflects an Alaskan lodge theme. It's beautiful and probably worth the price for those who can afford it.

Forget-Me-Not Lodge, 1540 Chena Road, ☎ (907) 474-0949. 10 rooms. Small but unusually attractive, the lodge is a cross between a hotel and a B&B. A few rooms are housed in Pullman sleeper cars. Full breakfast included.

Regency Fairbanks Hotel, 95 10th Avenue, ☎ (907) 452-3200 or (800) 348-1340. 130 rooms. $$$-$$$$. Full-service downtown hotel with attractive rooms and many amenities. Pricey, but still considerably less than the Princess.

River's Edge Resort, 4200 Boat Street, ☎ (907) 474-0286 or (800) 770-3343. 94 rooms. $$$. A nice place that's a little off the beaten path, the resort has motel-style units and riverside cabins with patios. The public areas are decorated in a gold rush era style.

Sophie Station Hotel, 1717 University Avenue, ☎ (907) 479-3650 or (800) 528-4916. 147 rooms. $$$. An all-suite hotel that provides excellent lodging and a reasonable value. The grounds are beautifully landscaped. Close to the airport. Free transportation is provided to the airport and train station.

Westmark Fairbanks, 813 Noble Street, ☎ (907) 456-7722 or (800) 544-0970. 242 rooms. $$$. Attractive and well-appointed hotel with a good restaurant. Transportation to airport and train station is provided.

> *TIP: On your way back to Anchorage keep a sharp lookout for weather conditions. It's always possible that a sought-after view of Mt. McKinley, which may have been obscured on the trip north, will now have opened up.*

The Matanuska Valley

The attractions in this section are much closer to Anchorage than Fairbanks but we've included them here because they are all located off of the direct route from Anchorage to Denali.

However, you can just as easily do them on the way north, or as a separate side trip from Anchorage itself.

The pretty Matanuska Valley is centered around the town of Palmer which is located on the Glenn Highway (Alaska 1). You reach it by branching off the main road between Anchorage and Denali just north of Wasilla. From there it is only a short ride into Palmer.

There are many farms within the Matanuska Valley. Due to the unusual summer growing conditions (up to 20 hours of sunshine daily), vegetables sometimes reach enormous sizes. Even 60-pound cabbages are not unusual here. Few farms are visible from the Glenn Highway, but you can get information and a good map at the **Visitor Information Center** in Palmer if you want to drive the back roads they can be found on. Giant vegetables are always on display in the attractive garden located outside the Visitor Center in the heart of town. You can also visit the **Matanuska Agricultural Experimental Farm**, seven miles southwest, where some of the larger specimens can be seen.

Palmer is the site of the Alaska State Fairgrounds. However, the most famous of Palmer's attractions may well be the **Musk Ox Farm**, Milepost 50 on the Glenn Highway, about two miles north of town, ☎ (907) 745-4151. This is an interesting opportunity to take a guided walk through the farm and come face to face with over a hundred of these large but very unhandsome beasts. It's the only domestic herd of musk ox in the world. You'll learn how their hair, qiviut, is woven into the rich cloth that is so sought after by discriminating shoppers. Qiviut is eight times warmer than wool and has 20 times the tensile strength, yet it is softer than fine silk and is ideal for knitting scarves and sweaters. Open daily from 9 am until 6 pm and the admission is $8.

Beyond the Cruise

A little farther to the east along the Glenn Highway is a fantastic view of the **Matanuska Glacier,** which measures some 27 miles in length and almost four miles across. There is also a trail that leads up to the edge of the glacier.

Upon returning to the town of Palmer you might also be interested in taking an approximately 20-mile side trip north via the Hatcher Pass Road to **Independence Mine State Historical Park.** This was once a booming gold mining town and you can visit some of the 15 well-preserved buildings from that time (the 1930s and '40s). The park itself is quite interesting and the surrounding area provides some lovely scenery on the drive to and from the former town. The park is open daily from 11:00 am until 7:00 pm; there is a per vehicle admission charge of $5.

That concludes our exploration of the interior. In summing up, keep in mind that a round-trip from Anchorage to Denali National Park requires at least two full days, with a third day usually necessary if you intend to use the shuttle bus in Denali. Another day or two is required to include Fairbanks. Package excursions sold as cruise add-ons take anywhere from two to seven days, depending upon their itinerary. Even those who plan to drive might want to see if they can arrange a one-way car rental and return via the Alaska railroad.

Other Alaskan Destinations

Alaska, with its immense spaces and inspiring natural terrain has lots more of interest to see than was included here. Size is one of the problems in getting to see much of Alaska and the remoteness is another. By comparison, every place mentioned so far is relatively easy to get to for cruise or Alaskan ferry passengers. The list that follows will serve as an outline of possible additional Alaskan destinations. Cruise passengers, especially those traveling with some of the larger Alaskan operators such as Princess or Holland America, should inquire as to the availability of add-on tours to some of these localities. Smaller operators will often be able to accommodate those interested in more far-flung or out-of-the-way places.

Alaska Peninsula & Aleutian Islands

Beginning with Katmai National Park and Preserve in the north and stretching far into the north Pacific, this seemingly endless stretch of islands and mainland is one of the most remote regions in all of Alaska. The area is liberally sprinkled with national parks and monuments and wildlife refuges. Getting to them is either by boat or air. Exploring the tiny main towns of Chignik, King Cove and Dutch John, with their colorful wooden houses and frontier atmosphere, is like visiting another world. All are connected by a branch of the Alaska Marine Highway system.

Nome

On the Seward Peninsula opposite the Russian far east, Nome is about 550 air miles from Anchorage. There are no road or regular ship connections to Nome, although once arriving in town there are a series of unpaved routes that lead into wilderness areas almost as far as the Bering Land Bridge National Preserve, a wildlife habitat. Air tours of the Preserve and other areas around Nome are the best way to get around. The Native American culture of Nome is colorful and interesting.

Beyond the Cruise

The North Slope

From Barrow to Prudhoe Bay, this 200-mile-long stretch of Arctic tundra will reveal few glimpses of civilization. Although the unpaved Dalton Highway is open to the public almost until Prudhoe Bay, for practical purposes, the only way to reach this region is by air. The towns are small and the Native American population makes for an interesting change of pace. Because of the large area covered most tours of the area are by air. Some people come this far north primarily to experience the "midnight sun" during the summer. The aurora borealis is often spectacular from this area.

Wrangell-St. Elias National Park & Preserve

Most of the vast parkland is back-country wilderness but there are two unpaved roads that each extend about 50 miles into the park's interior. You can get there by taking the Glenn Highway (Alaska 1) about 180 miles from Anchorage to Glennallen. From there, Alaska 1 skirts the edge of the park for some 75 miles before reaching one of the two roads into the park. The other park road is reached by going south from Glennallen for 65 miles via Alaska 4 and then Alaska 10. Besides the magnificent glacier and mountain scenery – many peaks in excess of 16,000 feet high – this vast park of more than eight million square miles (more than three times as large as Yellowstone and the largest in the National Park System) is also a wonderful wildlife refuge for animals large and small.

West Coast Gateways

Although Vancouver is still the primary departure point for cruises to Alaska, Seattle is becoming increasingly important. Even if you depart from Vancouver, there is a good chance that you'll still be flying into Seattle and then busing (or driving on your own) into Vancouver. These two cities are under 150 miles apart by super-highway and the trip can be made in less than three hours. Therefore, it is logical to consider both of these locations as gateway cities for our purposes.

While the British Columbia provincial capital of Victoria is not a gateway to your cruise in the same sense as Seattle and Vancouver, its proximity to the latter (connected by frequent ferry service) and the fact that it is such a lovely place make it a destination that simply should not be missed. These three cities and their environs certainly contain enough to fill up a major vacation in and of themselves. However, that sort of description is outside the scope of this book, so we're just going to cover the highlights.

If you don't plan on getting back to the Pacific Northwest, you should definitely consider tacking on a few more days to your trip to see Seattle and Vancouver, but also Victoria if you can manage it. Any and all make a fantastic introduction or finale to your trip. The next chapter provides a "highlight" tour for each of these cities – that is, a tour that can be reasonably accomplished in one full day of sightseeing for each. For those with more time or who plan to visit only one city, we'll list some additional worthwhile attractions. Cruise lines have several different options for seeing these cities by guided tour, but we strongly recommend a little individual travel here.

Some Alaska cruises depart from San Francisco or Los Angeles, but we don't consider either as a gateway. This is because of

Beyond the Cruise

the amount of time lost before reaching Alaska as well as the fact that the number of cruises to Alaska departing from these locations is rather limited.

Seattle

Recognized as one of the most livable cities in the United States, Seattle is also one of the nicest to visit. The "Emerald City" is tucked onto a narrow strip of land between Puget Sound to the west and Lake Washington to the east. Across the sound are the dramatic Olympic Mountains and many lush, green islands, all connected to Seattle via a comprehensive ferry system. The Cascade Range forms a backdrop to the city's east and on clear days Mt. Rainier is visible. Seattle is very hilly and that, combined with its location on the water, will remind many visitors of San Francisco.

THE 1-DAY HIGHLIGHT TOUR

The downtown area runs several blocks inland from the waterfront, rising steeply uphill as one walks away from the harbor. In many ways Seattle's physical setting is comparable to that of San Francisco, although the romanticism of the latter hasn't caught on in images of Seattle. Excellent views of the Sound and its constant vessel traffic can be had from virtually any street corner from 2nd Avenue upward. The downtown core is filled with impressive skyscrapers and those who appreciate modern architecture will enjoy a stroll through this part of the city.

The historic area is to the immediate south of the central business district. Within this area are such attractions as the **Klondike Gold Rush National Historic Park** and **Pioneer Square**. If the former sounds familiar to you, that's because it is the southern unit of the same park located in Skagway. Seattle was the initial departure point for most prospective

Klondike adventurers and their history is well documented in the Seattle section of the park. Pioneer Square surrounds the park and contains buildings from Seattle's early days, but not originals since the town was leveled by fire in the late 1880s. Rundown until a few years ago, Pioneer Square has been turned into a fashionable area of shops and restaurants. Within this district is the **Smith Tower**, one of the first skyscrapers west of Chicago. The 42-story white structure has intricate carvings.

The most important downtown attractions are near to or along the waterfront Alaskan Way centered around the vicinity of Piers 59. Begin at the **Pike Place Market**. The market was once destined for the wrecker's ball, but local citizens fought to preserve the colorful and boisterous area. Besides shopping for fresh produce and fish, residents and visitors alike flock to the market for the fine restaurants, street musicians and unique atmosphere. The market is connected to the waterfront by the **Pike Place Hill Climb**, a series of paths, stairways and elevators. An old-fashioned trolley runs along Alaskan Way and is not only fun to ride, but can save a lot of walking. Among the many attractions in the vicinity of Pier 59 are the **Omnidome Film Experience** and the **Seattle Aquarium**, one of the finest in the country. Exhibits concentrate on the marine life of Puget Sound, but also feature a Pacific coral reef display. Upon returning from the waterfront you can visit the excellent **Seattle Art Museum**, located near the Pike Place Market.

From downtown take the **Monorail** for a quick ride to the **Seattle Center**. Site of the 1962 World's Fair, the grounds now contain the **Space Needle, Pacific Science Center, Experience Music Project** and other attractions. No visit to Seattle is complete without a trip to the observation deck of the futuristic looking 605-foot-high Space Needle, now a symbol of the city. The deck is at the 520-foot level and provides a

Beyond the Cruise

sweeping panorama of the city, Puget Sound and the Olympic and Cascade Mountain Ranges. There are also two revolving restaurants. The Science Center contains various galleries devoted to different areas of scientific inquiry. There is also a children's museum and amusement park in Seattle Center.

Northeast of downtown is the famous **Lake Washington Ship Canal** and **Hiram M. Chittenden Locks**. Visitors can watch the hundreds of small boats passing through the locks connecting Lakes Union and Washington with Puget Sound. A glass-enclosed underground viewing area along fish ladders allows visitors to observe trout and salmon making their upstream run. Summer is the best time to do this. Also on the grounds of the complex is an attractive botanical garden with more than 500 plant and shrub species. Guided and self-guided tours of the area are offered.

All of these sights will, unfortunately, have to get the quick treatment if you have only a single day. Much more time can be devoted to them (as well as the places listed below) if you can spare the extra day or two.

OTHER ATTRACTIONS

If you have additional time or want to substitute some of the suggested attractions in the highlight tour, among the numerous other worthwhile stops in Seattle are:

Downtown/Central Area – Various harbor tours or boat ride to Blake Island Marine State Park; Bill Speidel Underground Tours; Maritime Heritage Center.

South – Safeco Field (stadium tours); Museum of Flight, and a scenic drive around West Seattle to Alki Point (where Seattle was originally founded).

North – The University of Washington Arboretum and campus, including its several museums and galleries, the most noteworthy of which is the Burke Museum; Discovery Park; Nordic Heritage Museum; Woodland Park Zoo; the eclectic neighborhood of Fremont.

East – Cross the two floating bridges over Lake Washington that connect Seattle with Mercer Island and the large community of Bellevue.

Vancouver

In a physical setting that matches and probably exceeds that of Seattle, Vancouver is the third-largest city in Canada. On a fjord called the Burrard Inlet, it is edged to the north and east by perpetually snow-capped mountains. The downtown area is on a small piece of land that juts out into the inlet. It's a city of parks and year-round flowers due to the mild and wet climate. Most downtown attractions are close to one another, but a modern light-rail rapid transit system will also be of help in getting around town.

THE 1-DAY HIGHLIGHT TOUR

The downtown area contains fine shopping along a pedestrian mall and the usual impressive office buildings. But the more interesting areas of the city center are its historical and ethnic communities, notably **Gastown**, **Robsonstrasse**, and **Chinatown.** Gastown occupies the site of the original settlement of Vancouver and contains many restored buildings, shops, and restaurants. Robsonstrasse (actually Robson Street) testifies to the important influence of German immigrants in the area, and Chinatown is home to one of the largest Asian communities in North America.

Vancouver has one of the world's greatest city parks. **Stanley Park** contains miles of scenic drives and numerous paths for walking and bicycling. It is also noted for its extremely fine collection of totem poles, an aquarium, floral clock and out-

Beyond the Cruise

standing views of the city skyline, Burrard Inlet and mountains to the north. From here you'll be able to gaze down upon your cruise ship docked at **Canada Place**.

South of downtown is the outstanding **Queen Elizabeth Park and Bloedel Conservatory**. The park contains one of the most colorful botanic gardens you're likely to see on the North American mainland. The conservatory is a unique domed structure housing species that wouldn't adapt well to Vancouver's cooler climate. Pathways thread through the gardens and a hilltop vantage point affords views not only of the entire garden, but the city beyond.

Some of the city's outstanding attractions are located in North Vancouver, just across the Burrard Inlet via one of two bridges connecting this community with Vancouver proper. Boats provide another means of transportation between the two locations. **Capilano Canyon** and **Lynn Canyon** are both natural gorges with lush vegetation and are spanned by swinging foot bridges which provide quite a thrill when you wobbly-walk across them – don't worry, they're perfectly safe! Capilano Canyon bridge is longer, but Lynn Canyon hangs over a rockier and more interesting terrain. Lynn Canyon is a public park with no entrance fee; Capilano Canyon is a fee-charging private enterprise. You don't have to visit both, especially if time is running short.

Not far from Capilano Canyon is **Grouse Mountain Skytram**. A large cable car whisks you to the top of Grouse Mountain for an extraordinary view of Vancouver. It's spectacular by day or at night when the lights of the city twinkle beneath you.

OTHER ATTRACTIONS

Again, we'll provide a listing of more sights to see for those with additional time.

Downtown – The lookout at Harbor Centre (observation deck atop an office tower, also contains a shopping promenade); BC Place (ultra-modern domed stadium); Vancouver Art Gallery; Canadian Crafts Museum; Science World. Near to downtown is Chinatown and the Dr. Sun Yat-Sen Classical Chinese Garden.

West – Scenic drive around the peninsula through the University of British Columbia with stops at the Nitobe Japanese Gardens, Maritime Museum, and the Vancouver Museums, including the Pacific Space Center.

East – Exhibition Park (contains various amusement areas, especially good for those traveling with children).

North – Drive to top of Mt. Seymour Provincial Park (a good substitute for Grouse Mountain Skytram since the view is similar). Do not attempt the drive during inclement weather.

South – Vandusen Botanical Gardens.

Victoria

The provincial capital is located on Vancouver Island, the largest island on the Pacific coast. The city of Vancouver is on the mainland, which may be somewhat confusing to the geographically uninitiated. It's a small city compared to its mainland neighbor, but that's one of its attractions. Nowhere else in the world, outside of England itself, offers more of an "old English" atmosphere. Afternoon tea at the elegant Empress Hotel is still a time-honored tradition. It's so popular that reservations are required. Victorian-era street lights with hanging flower baskets adorn the major streets.

The trip to Victoria is half the fun of the visit. Large car ferries leave hourly during the summer from the town of Tsawwassen, 15 miles south of downtown Vancouver via

Route 17. The crossing via BC Ferries takes about 95 minutes and threads through small islands near Vancouver Island. It's a most pleasant ride. You leave your car below and sit in enclosed lounges or on deck to admire the passing scenery. For those not renting a car, direct bus service from Vancouver to Victoria is provided. The buses roll on and off the ferries just as cars do. The ferry dock for Victoria is in the small hamlet of Swartz Bay, 20 miles north of the center of Victoria.

THE 1-DAY HIGHLIGHT TOUR

The primary downtown attractions are all within close proximity to one another. The highlight is a tour of the provincial **Parliament**, a stately and impressive edifice with beautiful grounds that contain a statue of Queen Elizabeth. (The building is illuminated at night with a fairy tale-like display of lights). The adjacent **Royal British Columbia Museum** houses an outstanding collection of exhibits devoted to the human and natural history of the province. Lifelike dioramas of wildlife and native villages are the focal points.

The **Undersea Gardens** at the waterfront are contained in a white flower-bedecked structure resembling a submarine. You look through windows into the harbor and see a wide variety of colorful and sometimes unusual marine wildlife. There are also tank displays and feeding demonstrations. Outside the gardens is a nice view of the harbor and surrounding government buildings. A stroll through this colorful area leads to the regal **Empress Hotel**, whose ornate interior is worth a look.

The highlight of any visit to Victoria is a journey some 12 miles north to the community of Brentwood, home of the renowned **Butchart Gardens**. A former rock quarry, this large area has been turned into one of the most stunning sights in the world. The color is dazzling and the imaginative manner in which the flowers are displayed enhances the beauty. Pathways wind their way through the rolling landscape. The grounds contain several restaurants. You should time your trip to Victoria to arrive at the gardens in the late afternoon. This way you can enjoy them in the daylight, have dinner and stay for the illumination at nightfall. It's a spectacular sight. While you're waiting there is entertainment, which varies from one day to another. In summer there is an excellent fireworks display on certain evenings.

OTHER ATTRACTIONS

Suggestions for those who wish to see more.

Within Victoria – Miniature World; Royal London Wax Museum; Beacon Hill Park; Craigdarroch Castle; Crystal Garden; Maritime Museum of British Columbia; Olde English Village, including Anne Hathaway's Cottage.

Nearby – Fort Rodd Hill National Historic Park; Royal Roads University (set on a former estate); and the Canadian Forces Base Esquimalt. The latter has tours of the base and a naval and military museum. To the north, in the vicinity of Butchart Gardens are the Victoria Butterfly Gardens.

This brief introduction to the gateway cities is certainly not all-inclusive. While it's more than adequate for a day or two, anyone planning a comprehensive trip to this area should seek additional information, especially for the multitude of scenic attractions within a day's drive of Vancouver and Seattle. The largely wild interior of Vancouver Island also presents possibilities for a back-country vacation.

Addenda

Additional Sources of Information

State of Alaska

Alaska Division of Tourism
PO Box 110801
Juneau AK 99811-0801
☎ (907) 465-2010
www.commerce.state.ak.us/tourism

Interior Road Conditions Report
☎ (907) 456-7623

Transportation

Air

Air Canada
☎ (800) 776-3000
www.aircanada.ca

Alaska Airlines
☎ (800) 426-0333
www.alaskaair.com

America West
☎ (800) 235-9292
www.americawest.com

Continental
☎ (800) 525-0280
www.continental.com

Delta Air Lines
☎ (800) 221-1212
www.delta-air.com

Northwest Airlines
☎ (800) 225-2525
www.nwa.com

United Airlines
☎ (800) 241-6522
www.ual.com

Ferry

Department of Transportation & Public Facilities
Division of Marine Highways
PO Box 25535
Juneau AK 99802-5535
☎ (800) 642-0066
www.dot.state.ak.us/external/amhs

Train

Alaska Railroad Corporation
PO Box 107500
Anchorage AK 99510
☎ (800) 544-0552
www.state.ak.us/local/akpages/commerce/
arrc.htm

White Pass & Yukon Railroad
PO Box 435
Skagway AK 99840
☎ (800) 343-7373
www.whitepassrailroad.com

Public Lands

General
Alaska Public Lands Information Center
605 W. 4th Avenue
Anchorage AK 99501
☎ (907) 271-2737
www. nps.gov/aplic
(All US federal recreational lands can also be accessed
through www.recreation.gov)

Addenda

Alaska Public Lands Information Center
250 Cushman Street
Fairbanks AK 99701
☎ (907) 445-0514
See Anchorage listing above for web sites

Alaska State Parks
3601 C Street, Suite 200
Anchorage AK 99503-5929
☎ (907) 269-8400
www.dnr.state.ak.us/parks

Denali National Park & Preserve
Superintendent
Denali National Park
PO Box 9
Denali Park AK 99755
☎ (907) 683-2294
www.nps.gov/dena

Glacier Bay National Park
Superintendent
Glacier Bay National Park
PO Box 140
Gustavus AK 99826
☎ (907) 697-2230
www.nps.gov/glba

Kenai Fjords National Park
Superintendent
Kenai Fjords National Park
PO Box 1727
Seward AK 99664
☎ (907) 224-3175
www.nps.gov/kefj

Misty Fjords National Monument
Supervisor
Misty Fjords National Monument
3031 Tongass
Ketchikan AK 99901
☎ (907) 225-2148

Chugach National Forest
Forest Service Supervisor
Chugach National Forest
3301 C Street, Suite 300
Anchorage AK 99503
☎ (907) 271-2500
www.fs.fed.us/r10/chugach

Tongass National Forest
Forest Service Supervisor
Tongass National Forest
101 Egan Drive
Juneau AK 99801
☎ (907) 586-8751
www.fs.fed.us/r10/tongass

Alaska Localities

Addenda

Anchorage
Anchorage Visitor Information Center
546 W. 4th Avenue
Anchorage AK 99501
☎ (907) 274-3531;
(907) 276-3200 for pre-recorded information on
Anchorage current events
www.anchorage.net

Fairbanks
Fairbanks Visitor Information Center
550 First Avenue
Fairbanks AK 99701
☎ (800) 327-5774
www.explorefairbanks.com

Haines
Haines Visitor Center
PO Box 530
Haines AK 99827-0530
☎ (800) 458-3579
www.alaskainfo.org/haines

Homer
Homer Visitor Information Center
PO Box 541-VG
Homer AK 99603-0541
☎ (907) 235-5300
www.homeralaska.com

Juneau
Juneau Visitor Information Center
134 Third Street
Juneau AK 99801
☎ (907) 586-2201
www.alaskainfo.org/juneau

Ketchikan
Ketchikan Convention & Visitors Bureau
131 Front Street
Ketchikan AK 99901
☎ (907) 225-6166
www.Visit-Ketchikan.com

Seward
Seward Chamber of Commerce & Visitors Bureau
PO Box 749
Seward AK 99664
☎ (907) 224-3046
www.seward.net/chamber

Sitka
Sitka Convention & Visitors Bureau
PO Box 1226
Sitka AK 99835
☎ (907) 747-5940
www.alaskainfo.org/sitka

Skagway
Skagway Convention & Visitors Bureau
PO Box 415
Skagway AK 99840
☎ (907) 983-2855
www.skagway.org

Valdez
Valdez Convention & Visitors Bureau
Box 1603
Valdez AK 99686
☎ (800) 770-5954
www.vacationalaska.com/alaska/valdez

Wrangell
Wrangell Chamber of Commerce/Visitors Center
PO Box 49
Wrangell AK 99929
☎ (800) 367-9745
www.ilovealaska.com/alaska/wrangell

Addenda

Cruise Lines

Carnival Cruise Lines
Carnival Place
3655 NW 87th Avenue
Miami FL 33178-2428
☎ (800) 327-9501
www.carnival.com

Celebrity Cruises
5201 Blue Lagoon Drive
Miami FL 33126
☎ (800) 437-3111
www.celebritycruises.com

Crystal Cruises
2049 Century Park East, Suite 1400
Los Angeles CA 90067
☎ (800) 446-6620
www.crystalcruises.com

Holland America Line
300 Elliott Avenue West
Seattle WA 98119
☎ (800) 426-0327
www.hollandamerica.com

Norwegian Cruise Line
95 Merrick Way
Coral Gable FL 33134
☎ (800) 327-7030
www.ncl.com

Princess Cruise Line
10100 Santa Monica Blvd.
Los Angeles CA 90067-4189
☎ (800) PRINCESS
www.princess.com

Radisson Seven Seas Cruises
600 Corporate Drive, Suite 410
Fort Lauderdale, FL 33334
☎ (800) 285-1835
www.rssc.com

Royal Caribbean Cruises, Ltd.
1050 Caribbean Way
Miami FL 33132
☎ (800) 327-6700
www.rccl.com

Small Ship Operators

World Explorer Cruises
550 Montgomery Street, Suite 1400
San Francisco CA 94111
☎ (800) 854-3835
www.wecruise.com

Alaska Sightseeing/Cruise West
700 Fourth & Battery Building
Seattle WA 98121
☎ (800) 666-7375
www.cruisewest.com

Clipper Cruise Line
7711 Bonhomme Avenue
St. Louis MO 63105
☎ (800) 325-0010
www.clippercruise.com

Glacier Bay Tours & Cruises
226 2nd Avenue West
Seattle WA 98119
☎ (800) 451-5952
www.glacierbaytours.com

Addenda

Linblad Expeditions
640 Fifth Avenue
New York NY 10019
☎ (800) EXPEDITION
www.expeditions.com

Tour Operators

Note: Mailing addresses of tour operators are
not an indication of departure point.

Alaska Highway Cruises
3805 108th Avenue NE, Suite 204
Bellevue WA 98004-7613
☎ (800) 323-5757
www.reservation.cruise-flight-hotel.com

Alaska Sightseeing
543 West 4th Avenue
Anchorage AK 99501
☎ (800) 770-1305
www.cruisewest.com

Far North Tours
PO Box 102873-VG
Anchorage AK 99510-2873
☎ (800) 478-7480

Gray Line of Alaska
300 Elliott Avenue West
Seattle WA 98119
☎ (800) 478-6388
www.graylinealaska.com
(Anchorage office is located at 745 N. 4th Avenue,
☎ (907) 277-5581)

Kenai Fjord Tours
513 West 4th Avenue
Anchorage AK 99501
☎ (800) 478-8068
www.kenaifjords.com

Major Marine Tours
411 West 4th Avenue
Anchorage AK 99501
☎ (800) 764-7300
www.majormarine.com

Midnight Sun River Runners
PO Box 211561-VG
Anchorage AK 99521-1561
☎ (800) 825-7238
www.sinbad.net/~msrr

Princess Tours
See *Princess Cruises*

Westours
See *Holland America Line*

Addenda

Major Hotel Chains in Alaska

Best Western
☎ (800) 528-1234
www.bestwestern.com
*Located in Anchorage, Homer, Juneau, Ketchikan, Seward,
Soldotna and Wasilla.*

Super 8
☎ (800) 800-8000
www.super8.com
*Located in Anchorage, Fairbanks, Juneau, Ketchikan and
Sitka.*

Westmark
☎ (800) 544-0970
www.westmarkhotels.com
*Located in Anchorage, Beaver Creek, Dawson City,
Fairbanks, Juneau, Ketchikan, Skagway, Sitka, Tok, Valdez
and Whitehorse.*

Major Car Rental Companies

Alamo
☎ (800) 327-9633
www.goalamo.com

Avis
☎ (800) 331-1212
www.avis.com

Budget
☎ (800) 527-0700
www.budgetg.com/home

Hertz
☎ (800) 654-3131
www.hertz.com

National
☎ (800) 227-7368
www.nationalcar.com

Thrifty
☎ (800) 367-2277
www.thrifty.com

*Note: Major car rental companies may be hard to locate in the
smaller Inside Passage communities, such as Skagway, Juneau,
Sitka, etc. Check the Yellow Pages for the name and number of local operators.*

TIP: In Anchorage, local companies often offer lower rates than the national chains. Try one of the following: Affordable Car Rental, ☎ (907) 243-3370; Alaska Car & Van Rental, ☎ (800) 243-4832; U-Save Auto Rental, ☎ (800) 254-8728.

Gateway Cities

Seattle
Seattle/King County Convention/Visitors Bureau
800 Convention Place, Gallery One
Seattle WA 98101
☎ (206) 461-5840
www.seeseattle.org

Vancouver
Vancouver Travel InfoCenter
2000 Burrard Street, Plaza Level
Vancouver BC V6C 3L6
☎ (604) 683-2000
www.tourism-vancouver.org

Victoria
Victoria Travel InfoCenter
812 Wharf Street
Victoria BC V8W 1T3
☎ (250) 953-2033
www.travel.victoria.bc.ca

BC Ferries
BC Ferries
1112 Fort Street
Victoria BC V8V 4V2
☎ (250) 386-3431
www.bcferries.bc.ca

Addenda

An important note on Web addresses:

Whenever an "official" web site exists for a particular locality, tour service or business, we have listed the address of that site. However, in those cases where there is no official site, we have listed what we believe to be is the best available site for information on that locality or business.

Index

Index

Index

Index

www.hunterpublishing.com

 Hunter's full range of guides to all corners of the globe is featured on our exciting website. You'll find guidebooks to suit every type of traveler, no matter what their budget, lifestyle, or idea of fun.

Adventure Guides – There are now over 40 titles in this series, covering destinations from Costa Rica and the Yucatán to Tampa Bay & Florida's West Coast, New Hampshire and the Alaska Highway. Complete information on what to do, as well as where to stay and eat, *Adventure Guides* are tailor-made for the active traveler, with a focus on hiking, biking, canoeing, horseback riding, trekking, skiing, watersports, and all other kinds of fun.

Alive Guides – This ever-popular line of books takes a unique look at the best each destination offers: fine dining, jazz clubs, first-class class hotels and resorts. In-margin icons direct the reader at a glance. Top-sellers include: *The Cayman Islands, St. Martin & St. Barts,* and *Aruba, Bonaire & Curaçao*.

Our *Rivages Hotels of Character & Charm* books are top sellers, with titles covering France, Spain, Italy, Paris and Portugal. Originating in Paris, they set the standard for excellence with their fabulous color photos, superb maps and candid descriptions of the most remarkable hotels of Europe.

Our *Romantic Weekends* guidebooks provide a series of escapes for couples of all ages and lifestyles. Unlike most"romantic" travel books, ours cover more than charming hotels and delightful restaurants, with a host of activities that you and your partner will remember forever.

One-of-a-Kind travel books available from Hunter include *Best Dives of the Western Hemisphere; The Jewish Travel Guide; Golf Resorts; Cruising Alaska* and many more.